Evans Brothers Limited

Published by Evans Brothers Limited
2A Portman Mansions
Chiltern Street
London W1U 6NR
UK

First published in 2002

British Library Cataloguing in Publication Data
Monaghan, Tom
  The slave trade. - (Events and outcomes)
  1.Slave trade - Juvenile literature
  I.Title
  380.1'44

ISBN 0237523795

Edited by Rachel Norridge
Designed by Neil Sayer
Maps by Tim Smith
Consultant: Dr Kevin Shillington

Acknowledgements

Cover The Bridgeman Art Library **Background image** the art archive **p.6** the art archive **p.7** (top)
Mary Evans Picture Library (bottom) Peter Newark's American Pictures **p.8** the art archive **p.9** The
Bridgeman Art Library **p.11** (top) the art archive (bottom) Mary Evans Picture Library **p.12** the art
archive **p.14** (middle) Mary Evans Picture Library (bottom) The Bridgeman Art Library **p.15** Mary
Evans Picture Library **p.16** (top) Mary Evans Picture Library (bottom) the art archive **p.17** (top) Mary
Evans Picture Library (bottom) The Bridgeman Art Library **p.18** (top) the art archive (bottom) The
Bridgeman Art Library **p.19** The Bridgeman Art Library **p.20** Mary Evans Picture Library **p.21** (top)
Mary Evans Picture Library (bottom) The Bridgeman Art Library **p.22** (top) Peter Newark's American
Pictures (bottom) Topham Picturepoint **p.23** (top) Mary Evans Picture Library (bottom) Peter Newark's
American Pictures **p.24** Mary Evans Picture Library **p.25** Mary Evans Picture Library **p.26** the art
archive **p.27** The Bridgeman Art Library **p.28** The Bridgeman Art Library **p.29** Mary Evans Picture
Library **p.30** Mary Evans Picture Library **p.32** Mary Evans Picture Library **p.33** Peter Newark's
American Pictures **p.34** Peter Newark's American Pictures **p.35** Peter Newark's American Pictures
p.37 Mary Evans Picture Library **p.38** Peter Newark's American Pictures **p.39** Mary Evans Picture
Library **p.40** The Bridgeman Art Library **p.41** The Bridgeman Art Library **p.42** (top) The Bridgeman
Art Library (bottom) Mary Evans Picture Library **p.43** the art archive **p.44** Mary Evans Picture Library
p.45 The Bridgeman Art Library **p.47** (top) The Bridgeman Art Library (bottom) The Bridgeman Art
Library **p.48** Mary Evans Picture Library **p.49** (top) Mary Evans Picture Library (bottom) Mary Evans
Picture Library **p.50** The Bridgeman Art Library **p.51** (top) Peter Newark's American Pictures (bottom)
the art archive **p.52** Mary Evans Picture Library **p.53** Mary Evans Picture Library **p.54** the art archive
p.55 (top) Mary Evans Picture Library (bottom) The Bridgeman Art Library **p.56** Mary Evans Picture
Library **p.57** (top) Mary Evans Picture Library (bottom) Peter Newark's American Pictures **p.58** The
Bridgeman Art Library **p.60** Mary Evans Picture Library **p.61** (top) Mary Evans Picture Library (bottom) The Bridgeman Art Library **p.62** The Bridgeman Art Library **p.63** (top) Peter Newark's American
Pictures (bottom) The Bridgeman Art Library **p.64** Mary Evans Picture Library **p.65** (top) Peter
Newark's American Pictures (bottom) Corbis **p.67** (top) Topham Picturepoint (bottom) Mary Evans
Picture Library **p.68** Topham Picturepoint **p.69** Mary Evans Picture Library **p.70** Topham
Picturepoint **p.71** Topham Picturepoint **p.72** Mary Evans Picture Library

CONTENTS

THE ORIGINS OF SLAVERY

This basalt stone tablet, dating from nearly 4,000 years ago, is inscribed with Hammurabi, the King of Babylon's code of law. Among its 300 laws, the code states that helping a slave to escape was to be punished by a death sentence; slaves who escaped but were recaptured could be executed.

Slavery in the Ancient World

Slavery is the enforced servitude of people to another person or group. A slave is regarded as someone's property through birth, purchase or capture. As a social and economic institution, slavery appears to have originated when humans abandoned hunting and gathering in favour of subsistence farming. Among early civilisations, references to slavery are recorded in the Babylonian code of Hammurabi, and in the Bible. Forms of slavery were known in ancient China, and slave labour was a fact of life in ancient Greece and Rome, where slaves worked on large estates and met the demand for domestic servants in towns and cities. Often, slaves were prisoners of war, the children of slave parents, children sold into slavery by free parents, or criminals condemned to servitude.

Slavery in Asia and Africa

Numerous types of servitude developed throughout the world to serve a range of purposes, from solving a chronic labour shortage to serving as victims of ritual sacrifice. As well as being employed as agricultural labourers and servants, some slaves were able to exercise considerable power as stewards who managed large estates in China. Some slaves were captured as young boys in southern Europe, and forcibly converted to Islam, before being given a rigorous military training by their African or Middle Eastern owners. These warriors were able to achieve high rank in the armies of some Islamic countries, although female slaves were more highly prized than males in some parts of Africa and the Middle East, since they often served as wives and concubines. In Africa, a trans-Saharan trade in captives for sale into slavery existed before, during and after the period of the transatlantic slave trade.

Slavery in Europe

Following the decline of the Roman Empire in the west, a prominent feature of European society was the large

number of agricultural slaves known as serfs. These slaves were bound by law to the land where they worked. Serfdom in various forms was a common form of agricultural labour and persisted until at least the nineteenth century in some parts of Europe. In areas of France, elements of serfdom survived until the French Revolution at the end of the eighteenth century when nobles renounced their feudal rights. Another form of forced labour or servitude in modern Europe was the custom of young apprentices or servants signing a contract that bound them to a master for a number of years in return for food and shelter and, possibly, learning a trade.

Russian serfs were not given their freedom until the second half of the nineteenth century, like so many slaves in the New World. Were the serfs' lives so very different from the lives of slaves in the Americas?

Slavery in the New World

Following the defeat of the Moors in Spain and Portugal in the fifteenth century, captured Muslims were enslaved by the victorious Christians. Soon, these prisoners of war were joined by slaves imported from Africa. A regular trade in slaves was established between the Guinea coast of Africa and the Iberian peninsular. Colonists cultivating sugar cane on Atlantic islands, such as Madeira and the Canaries, relied on a mixture of slave and free labour. In the sixteenth century, African slaves were transported to colonies in the Americas, marking the beginning of a transatlantic slave trade that would transform the history of West Africa, and play a huge part in the social and economic development of Western Europe and the Americas.

African captives landing at Jamestown, Virginia, in 1619.

EUROPE AND THE SLAVE TRADE

New World Colonies

The transatlantic slave trade developed in the sixteenth century as European states established colonies in South and Central America. In the last decade of the fifteenth century, following the discoveries of Christopher Columbus on his expeditions to the New World, the Spanish established colonies in the eastern half of Haiti, Cuba, other islands in the Caribbean and in what is known as South America. In 1500, Portugal took possession of Brazil, and it was to become their largest and most important colony in the Americas.

Colonisation continued early in the seventeenth century with the English taking over Barbados, Jamaica and several other Caribbean islands, while the French settled in Guadaloupe and Martinique. In order to exploit the economic potential of these colonies, the European colonial powers needed an extensive supply of labour. For example, where conditions were favourable, the Spanish and Portuguese had started to grow sugar cane to be processed and shipped back to Europe.

The harvesting and processing of sugar cane to produce sugar in its many forms became the focus of economic life on many Caribbean islands, such as Antigua.

Plantations were established in Brazil, Mexico, Paraguay, the Pacific coast of South America and islands in the Caribbean. They had also discovered that crops such as rice, citrus fruits, olives and tobacco grew well in these new colonies. Native inhabitants were pressed into service as forced labour, but many died of overwork, disease and hunger, or simply ran off into the forests. Free labour from Europe chose to live in urban areas where they were employed as craftsmen and artisans, or took to self-employment in agriculture because fertile land was abundant. The Spanish and Portuguese therefore decided to import slave labour from the Atlantic islands and mainland Africa to work on sugar plantations, coffee and cocoa estates, or in gold and silver mines.

European Consumers

Population growth and economic change had led to improved standards of living in European towns and cities. This increased consumer demand for plantation produce such as sugar, tobacco, coffee and cocoa. In response, colonists in the Americas enlarged their estates and purchased slave labour from Africa to increase the production of crops that commanded a high price from European traders. Therefore, growing consumer demand for colonial produce in European markets encouraged colonists to purchase more slaves to meet that demand.

The Spanish and Portuguese shipped huge numbers of African slaves across the Atlantic to work in colonies such as Cuba and Brazil. Next, the Dutch took advantage of their enormous banking and shipping resources to become financiers of the burgeoning slave trade. They supplied many of the slave ships required to transport tens of thousands of Africans to servitude in the New World.

The *Southall* frigate was one of many European vessels trading on the coast of West Africa in the seventeenth century. Its crew would have found African traders eager to obtain European goods in exchange for captives.

The French Colonies

The expansion of output in the French colonies did not occur until the last quarter of the eighteenth century, with the most dramatic development taking place in the colony of Saint-Domingue. From 1760, this French colony's sugar production expanded dramatically, and the colonists set about increasing their production of coffee and cotton by taking advantage of the terrain and soil of their island. The result of this expansion in plantation production was a huge increase in the number of slaves employed in the colony, and the proportion of African-born slaves within the total population of Saint-Domingue was greater than that of any other large colony in the Americas.

Triangular Trade

European governments were attracted to the economic benefits of possessing colonies in the New World, and sought to exploit the commercial advantages of using slave labour. Slavery and the trade in slaves proved to be major factors in the economic development of Europe's colonial powers. A lucrative long-distance transatlantic slave trade developed as a complex network of commercial enterprises. Contemporaries, however, identified a triangular trade. First, European goods such as alcohol, firearms and textiles were shipped from Europe to be traded for slaves in West Africa. Second, the slaves would then be shipped to South America or the Caribbean where they would be traded for staples such as sugar, tobacco, and later, raw cotton. Third, these products of the New World colonies were exported to Europe and sold for large profits. In reality, the trade was much more complex than this simple description. For example, in the eighteenth century, two out of every five slave ships sailed to and from ports in the Americas.

A map showing the eighteenth-century triangular transatlantic trade.

Great Britain
Europe
North America
Atlantic Ocean
Sugar, cotton, tobacco
Guns, cloth, pots, metal etc.
West Indies
Slaves
West Africa
South America
Slaves

The Extent of the Trade

During the eighteenth century, European merchants controlled the transatlantic slave trade along a 1,000-mile stretch of the West African coast. At least ten million African captives were transported across the Atlantic between 1500 and the end of the nineteenth century. By the end of the eighteenth century, two African captives had crossed the Atlantic for every European colonist who had sailed to the New World. Half of those Africans were transported in the eighteenth century, and most were carried on Portuguese, British or French vessels, with assistance from Spanish, Dutch, Danish and Swedish ships. A significant proportion of the Portuguese and British

In the late seventeenth century, European slave traders could spend months sailing up and down the African coast. They would row ashore at regular intervals to meet chiefs and traders who could supply them with captives to fill their holds before they set off on the Middle Passage.

Commerce.

Documents, like this list of slaves exported from Cameroon at the end of the eighteenth century, are often the only clue to the ethnic origin of the millions of captives who were transported to the New World.

ships sailed from colonies in the Americas. Some British slave traders operated out of ports in New England and Barbados. They supplied colonies in the Caribbean and on the mainland of North and South America, while Portuguese traders sailed from Bahia in Brazil and supplied their own colonies. In total, Brazil and the Caribbean bought 90 per cent of the African captives who survived the journey, known as the 'Middle Passage', from West Africa to the West Indies.

During the eighteenth century, slaves accounted for about 70 per cent of the total population of the Caribbean region, and on those European colonies where sugar cane was the main crop, the slave population could account for nearly 90 per cent of the total population. The size of the slave population in Europe's American colonies reached its peak at the end of the eighteenth century, although the number of slaves in the former European colonies of Brazil and the United States of America continued to grow until the 1840s and 1850s, respectively.

Slave caravans were crossing North Africa long before the Europeans took an interest in the trade. European slave traders were able to take advantage of existing trade routes and African merchants' contacts and expertise.

The Effects in Africa

In the years before the transatlantic slave trade developed, the Europeans had bought African slaves who had been transported by slave traders across the Sahara region to North Africa. As the number of captives being transported across the Atlantic Ocean grew, trade between Africans and Europeans stimulated change and growth in the economy of West Africa.

African farming was adapted to grow crops used to provision the slave ships. The areas that supplied agricultural produce for the transatlantic trade were not always the same as those that supplied slaves. Captives were taken from almost the whole area of West Africa, but crops were supplied from areas with reliable transport links to the trading stations on the coast. The reason for this was the high cost of transport in West Africa. Marching captives to the coast presented few problems, but agricultural produce had to be transported, either by water or on porters' heads. Since the price of a single captive was roughly equivalent to that of a ton of palm oil (which would require about 60 porters to transport it any distance), it was not profitable to produce palm oil or any other agricultural produce for export unless it was grown close to the coast or a navigable river.

Captives were transported long distances to reach the markets and trading centres on the west coast of Africa.

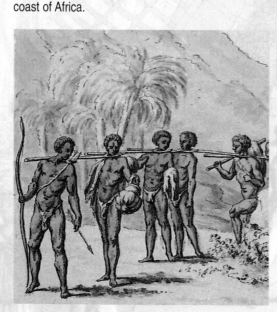

Slave Trading Centres in Africa

On the coast of West Africa, as many as 75 per cent of African captives embarked from Luanda, the Zaire or Congo River, the Niger Delta, and the Bight of Benin. Coastal states developed transport and trading networks that were able to supply small trading centres or larger stone trading forts with captives from the interior. European slave traders expected supplies to be regular and reliable. At some trading sites, African merchants developed road and river networks from the interior to the coast. One British slave trader, Thomas Clarkson, described in 1789 how he accompanied African traders as their fleet of canoes,

called at villages as we passed, and purchased our slaves fairly; but in the night they made several excursions on the banks of the river ... broke into the villages ... and seized men, women and children.

Over time, the focus of the slave trade moved south, and West Central Africa was the centre of the trade in its final decades. When the British attempted to enforce a ban on the transatlantic slave trade in the nineteenth century, traders south of the equator continued to supply Brazil and Cuba from Angola and Mozambique. As colonies developed and required more forced labour, some regions of Africa supplied the bulk of slaves shipped to particular colonies.

The Portuguese colony of Brazil received most of its slaves from Angola and the Bight of Benin, also known as the Slave Coast. The French colony of Saint-Domingue took a large proportion of its captives from the Bight of Benin, too. The British colonies were supplied with captives from a wide range of regions, but the Bight of Biafra, the Gold Coast and Angola were the United Kingdom's main sources of slaves in the second half of the eighteenth century. The island of Cuba was unique in that the Spanish government allowed the colony to receive slave shipments from most European merchants and, as a result, no single African region supplied more than one-third of Cuba's slaves.

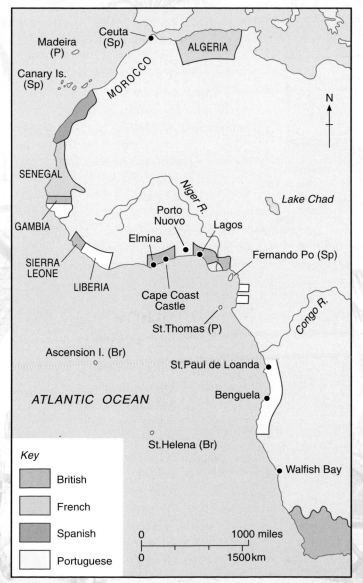

A map of West Africa, showing the location of the chief slave-trading regions.

Key

- British
- French
- Spanish
- Portuguese

0 — 1000 miles
0 — 1500 km

13

European Trade with Africa

European traders tried to cheat the Africans at every turn. Alcohol was diluted with water, gunpowder barrels had false bottoms, and pieces were cut out of rolls of cloth. Chiefs and kings stopped ruling by traditional laws and customs, and became greedy tyrants, taking advice from the slave traders' ruthless European agents. In the sixteenth century, King Affonso of the Kongo complained to the Portuguese that,

so great is the corruption and lawlessness that our country is being completely depopulated.

The vast majority of African children who were abducted by raiders would be unable to trace their parents or return to their home villages.

Tribal wars became more common, encouraged by the profits that could be made from the slave trade. Law and justice were corrupted as more and more crimes, no matter how small, were punished by enslavement. Thousands of villages were progressively deserted as a result of wars or raids to capture slaves.

Africans Supply Slaves

Some African states which had enslaved captives for many years, enslaved yet more people when the transatlantic slave trade developed. From the late seventeenth century, Ashanti (Asante) traded slaves and captives for European goods, such as cloth, alcohol and guns. It used these resources to make itself more powerful, and to start wars against its neighbours to acquire more captives. Another African kingdom that took advantage of the transatlantic slave trade was Dahomey. In the eighteenth century, the kings of Dahomey organised raids into neighbouring lands largely to capture prisoners to sell on to European traders. On a smaller scale, other kingdoms took part in the slave trade, venturing far inland to take captives to sell on to Europeans. In these coastal areas, native crafts died out, unable to compete with cheap European goods mass produced in factories.

This image of the King of Dahomey gives us some idea of the power and prestige of those African rulers who profited from the trade in African captives.

The Profits of Slave Labour

The transatlantic trade in human cargo, and the crops that slave labour produced, financed the building of new harbours and the construction of new shipyards in the British Isles. In turn, this led to increased orders for British factories producing goods for export to Africa and the American colonies. In the second half of the eighteenth century, Britain's major seaports made huge profits from transatlantic trade.

Slaves produced about 75 per cent of the total value of exports from the Americas traded in the Atlantic area in the seventeenth and eighteenth centuries. By the end of the eighteenth century, British industries producing for export markets that included the Americas were growing faster than those producing mainly for the domestic market. Liverpool merchants sent a petition to Parliament in 1788 that claimed that abolition of the slave trade would,

 ruin the property of the English merchants in the West Indies, diminish the public revenue and impair (weaken) the maritime strength of Great Britain.

Race Relations

Ethnic and religious differences between the European slave owners and their African slaves helped to legitimise master–slave relationships, and distinguish between those who could be forcibly enslaved and those who could not. Modern European slavery in the colonial era was characterised by its ethnic composition. Most slaves were African by birth, or the descendants of Africans who had been transported to European colonies in North and South America. Most slave owners were Europeans or their descendants.

Diverse conditions and traditions fostered variations between societies in the European colonies, both in terms of slavery and race relations, but it is true to say that slavery in Europe's American colonies was predicated on an unequal relationship between Europeans and non-Europeans. This inequality has had repercussions for race relations in the Atlantic world ever since.

In the eighteenth century, the ownership of slaves in Britain's American colonies provided a large labour force on plantations, and was a measure of wealth and prestige.

Xenophon's book on how to handle slaves reminds us that early Europeans took slavery for granted.

The brutal treatment of captives and the enslavement of prisoners came together in the use of slave gladiators in the arenas of the Roman Empire.

European Civilisation and Slavery

From ancient times, European states had exploited slave labour. Ancient attitudes towards Europeans who were enslaved were similar to those faced by African captives in the modern era. The Greek soldier Xenophon wrote a manual for slave owners, giving advice on how to select suitable slaves for employment on a large estate. In particular, he emphasised the qualities of intelligence, energy, loyalty and experience required by any slave in a position of responsibility.

The philosopher Plato, writing 2,500 years ago, believed that Greeks should not be enslaved by Greeks, but he did not conclude that slavery was unjust. Instead, he wrote that slavery should be restricted to foreigners or 'barbarians', and that the status of slave could be inherited from parents. At that stage in European civilisation, the idea had developed that those who were enslaved were inferior to their owners. The philosopher Aristotle, who was a pupil of Plato, wrote that:

From the hour of their birth some are marked out for subjection, others for rule.

Aristotle went so far as to suggest that it was the duty of superior Greeks to enslave inferior barbarians, in order that both groups could fulfil their true functions, to their mutual benefit.

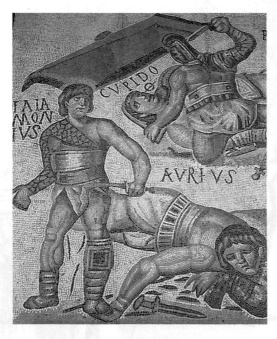

Ancient Rome

The Roman Empire swallowed up most of southern and western Europe, and most of North Africa. Slaves were imperial victims whose lives were held cheap by ruthless rulers who enjoyed absolute power over their imperial conquests. For centuries, the citizens of the Roman Empire demanded the deaths of thousands of slave gladiators each year for their entertainment, and tolerated the branding, burning, beating and mutilation of slaves by owners who believed that these humans were property, not people with civil rights. Roman ideas about government and society continued to influence European civilisation when the transatlantic slave trade developed.

Exploration and Oppression

The Portuguese and Spanish explorers who set sail for the New World across the Atlantic in the wake of Columbus in the 1490s, took for granted their right to enslave enemies and exploit forced labour. Mistakenly believing that they were exploring the Indies in South-East Asia, the explorers had called the people who lived on these islands 'Indians'. A more serious error was the failure of these explorers to appreciate the differences between their own European culture and beliefs, and those of the many peoples whom they encountered. The simple technology, hospitality and generosity of so many indigenous peoples were mistaken for signs of weakness, and the superiority of European civilisation was assumed at all times. Columbus described the inhabitants of the island that he named Hispaniola as being kind, peaceful and generous, but he noted in his journal that:

With fifty men they could all be subjected and made to do all that I wished.

An artist's impression of Peruvians from Lima, drawn about 1700. Three centuries later, archaeologists are still uncovering evidence of the achievements of the civilisations that inhabited the Americas before the arrival of Europeans in the fifteenth and sixteenth centuries.

European Violence

Contact between Europe and the New World led to death and misery on a huge scale. Within fifty years of Columbus setting foot on the island, it is estimated that the indigenous population of Hispaniola fell from approximately 300,000 to less than 1,000, due to disease, war and the mistreatment of captives. From the outset, servitude in the Americas would be characterised by cruelty and violence towards non-Europeans. By 1600, nearly one million African captives had been transported across the Atlantic. Most of these victims would meet a fate similar to that of the peoples whom they were being used to replace as forced labour. The development of Europe's transatlantic trade demanded a high price of captives who were exploited by traders who paid scant respect to the humanity of their victims.

Plantation records, government files, colonists' diaries and letters, and the accounts left by freed men and women describe the brutality that slave ownership encouraged and condoned.

THE MIDDLE PASSAGE

Coastal Trade

This image of two merchants on an island off Senegal is a reminder of how European slave traders developed close links with the Africans who supplied captives for the Middle Passage.

In Africa, most of the trade in captives was carried out at markets in the small trading factories or larger stone forts along the Atlantic coast. Where there were no proper harbour facilities, slave ships would sail up and down the coast collecting batches of captives who had been ferried to the ships in small boats and canoes.

Ships' captains had to inspect the captives to assess whether or not they would survive the voyage and make a good price in the slave markets in the New World. Some captains could spend four or five months plying their trade along the African coast until they had enough slaves to fill their holds.

The Middle Passage

The death rate among sailors involved in trade with Africa was very high. Since a significant proportion of the crew was likely to die from disease before they reached the Americas, crew levels could fall to dangerous levels. Slave ship captains had to be prepared to face storms and slave rebellions during what was known as the 'Middle Passage', and they needed as large a crew as possible to reach the slave markets on the other side of the Atlantic Ocean.

Two iron slave collars from around 1790. Archaeologists have found collars and chains small enough to fit children, or small adults.

Adult females made up about 25 per cent of the African captives who were forced into slavery in the Americas. For much of the eighteenth century, this ratio was largely determined by African supply conditions. Most captives were prisoners of war who were predominately male – female slaves were in much higher demand than males in Africa's domestic slave trade.

Children of both sexes made up roughly ten per cent of the slaves carried on the Middle Passage. Their numbers declined rapidly due to physical and sexual abuse aboard the vessels, and the ravages of smallpox, measles and other diseases that contributed to the high mortality rate among the younger captives. As there were so few female slaves in relation to males, the slave populations in most European colonies in the New World failed to reproduce their numbers.

Slave vessels setting sail on the Middle Passage from West African trading centres on the Gambia, Senegal and Sierra Leone rivers could take four to six weeks to complete the voyage. The passage could take several months from regions further east such as the Bight of Benin. Early in the history of the transatlantic slave trade, almost twenty per cent of African captives died during the Middle Passage. By the late eighteenth century, less than ten per cent of slaves died crossing the Atlantic, mainly due to improvements in hygiene and sanitation aboard ships.

Bills of Exchange

Slave ship captains and colonial merchants sold slaves to plantation owners in return for what were known as bills of exchange. These bills could be exchanged for return cargoes of plantation produce, but most slave vessels were not large enough to transport more than a fraction of the colonies' produce back to Europe. Instead, most colonial produce was carried on larger vessels known to the British as 'West Indiamen'. The smaller slave-carrying vessels did not play a significant part in the final leg of the triangular trade.

A Dutch ship landing captives at Jamestown in 1619. Most African captives were initially landed in the Caribbean and South America in the seventeenth and eighteenth centuries. Captives were carried in ships from most major European trading nations.

Slave Ships

Slave ships were small by modern standards, although they grew in size between the seventeenth and nineteenth centuries, from about 100 to 300 tons. Slave ships were rigged for speed and most carried between 200 and 300 captives. Contemporary diagrams of slave ships show how the captives were stacked below decks for the voyage. Often there were two levels, one above the other, on either side of the ship. Adult male captives had their right foot shackled to the left foot of the person on their right, and their left foot shackled to the right foot of the person on their left. The human cargo had little or no head room, making it impossible for them to sit up. Because they were chained, they found it difficult to change position. A doctor in 1790 noted that on overcrowded ships the captives,

complained of heat and want of air. Confinement in this situation was so injurious that he has known them to go down apparently in good health at night and found dead in the morning.

Women and children were not chained as a rule, but were liable to face physical and sexual abuse from sailors throughout the voyage.

Each day, when the weather permitted, some captives were taken on deck to exercise. Exercise, or 'dancing', was thought to prevent outbreaks of disease among the captives. When the sea was rough or the weather was inclement, the captives were kept below deck for long periods, and the sick and healthy, living and dead or dying, remained manacled together for days on end. Despite most ships carrying a medical assistant or doctor, outbreaks of dysentery were common due to the filthy conditions and lack of clean drinking water.

Deck plans for the slave ship *Brookes* which sailed out of Liverpool, England, at the end of the eighteenth century. Each male captive was allowed less than 1.8m by 40cm of room, so that the vessel could pack in 450 slaves.

Captive Resistance

Many African captives on the Middle Passage committed suicide. Some captives took the opportunity when exercising above deck to jump overboard and drown. Some appeared to lose the will to live and died from what was called 'fixed melancholy'. These captives would refuse to eat, and to discourage this form of resistance crews would beat these captives or torture them with thumbscrews. If this did not work, sailors would force-feed the captives by opening their jaws and forcing food into their mouths. Crews were known to use chisels to break the teeth of captives who resisted being force-fed. The slave traders were worried that if one captive refused to eat, others would follow suit and a large number of valuable Africans would die.

In fair weather, small groups of captives were brought up onto the main deck to dance during the voyage. This kept them fit and healthy, so they would fetch a good price when they reached the slave markets in the Americas.

Slave Rebellions

Europeans were always on guard against captives attempting to take control of the ship by killing the crew. One slave trader, John Newton, noted in his journal in 1753 that:

 I was at first continually alarmed with the slaves' almost desperate attempts to make attacks upon us.

Rebellions were most likely to occur when ships were off the African coast, before they set sail across the Atlantic. Most uprisings were put down ruthlessly by the European crews, but there were a few occasions when captives took control of the vessel on which they had been held captive. In 1742, the British vessel *Mary* was driven ashore on the River Gambia by the local people, and the captives on board seized the opportunity to kill most of the crew before escaping. However, the success of these captives was the exception rather than the rule.

A contemporary illustration showing the death of Captain Ferrer of the *Amistad*, when the captives seized control of the ship. The future of the captives aboard the *Amistad* led to a legal battle in the USA courts between the ship's owners and abolitionists.

The sale of African captives could take place aboard the slave ship, on a beach, or in a large sea port. This seventeenth-century Dutch auction of African slaves took place ashore in New Amsterdam (later New York).

Preparations For Sale

Having completed the voyage across the Atlantic, slave traders were determined to present their African captives to potential purchasers in the best possible condition. The captives who had survived the voyage were washed and fed for several days. Males were shaved and older captives had their grey hair dyed to make it more difficult to guess their age. Often, their skin was rubbed with palm oil to give their bodies a healthy sheen. Older or less healthy individuals might not attract any bids from colonists or their agents. They could be taken on to other islands where they could be put up for sale until they attracted a buyer, but sometimes these 'refuse' slaves were left to die of neglect, unattended at the quayside of the port where they had disembarked.

This branding iron was used to mark and identify slaves on arrival.

Slave Sales

The captives could be sold aboard the ship, soon after it arrived, or at a public auction ashore. In some ports, the captains of slave ships handed their human cargo over to agents for the vessels' owners. These agents inspected the captives as if they were livestock, checking limbs and teeth for defects, before advertising the place and time of the slave sale. Captives would be listed for sale by sex, approximate age and sometimes provenance or geographic origin, if known. In Spanish and Portuguese colonies, newly-arrived slaves would be branded with a red hot iron to indicate that they had been imported legally.

In the Caribbean, captives were often sold through a 'scramble' when prospective purchasers and their associates ran forward and claimed those captives whom they wanted to buy at an agreed price. Despite attempts to present new arrivals as fit and healthy, many colonists avoided buying captives who had just completed the Middle Passage since they could be carrying infectious diseases that threatened the existing slave population. Some colonists were not

When they were sold, captives would be separated from their fellow victims who had accompanied them on the Middle Passage, and they would be given a European name in place of their African name.

prepared to train recently arrived captives, who had to be acclimatised to their new environment and taught the skills of plantation labourers. Although some colonists were prepared to wait until newly-purchased slaves had recovered from the effects of the Atlantic crossing, many put new arrivals to work at once, especially if they were purchased at harvest time when labour was in short supply.

Many African captives were bought in Barbados and the Leeward Islands by slave traders who shipped them to the North American mainland, where they were sold either to colonists, or to other traders who sold them on to slave owners in the interior of the colonies. Charleston in South Carolina was the main port of direct entry for slaves in North America during the eighteenth century. Here, ships carrying captives had to wait outside the port at Sullivan Island for ten days. If the slaves aboard any ship turned out to be suffering from smallpox, the ship would be quarantined for at least four weeks.

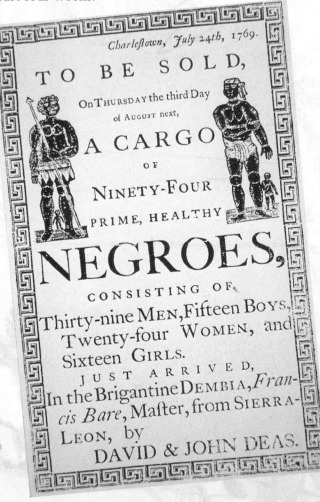

A poster advertising a slave auction of captives from Sierra Leone in Charleston, South Carolina, 1769.

The European Enlightenment

The term 'Enlightenment' refers to the changes in attitudes and beliefs that began in Europe around 300 years ago. European scientists, philosophers and political commentators in the eighteenth century, many known as *philosophes*, were united in the belief that rational, critical study and analysis should be applied in all matters. Many criticised political, social and economic practices that appeared to be irrational, such as superstitious religion or tyrannical rulers. They argued that the rational or reasoned foundation of government should be the welfare or well-being of the governed, who had 'natural rights' such as the right to fight against tyranny. These ideas developed at a time when Europeans were reaping the benefits of employing millions of slaves in the Americas. Rousseau, in his *Social Contract* (1762), wrote that:

 Man was born free, but everywhere he is in chains.

Revolutionary Ideals

At the time of the American Revolution, slavery and the slave trade remained key elements of economic prosperity in a large number of the colonies, united in their fight against British rule. In their Declaration of Independence, the American colonists included the enlightened phrase:

All men are created equal.

Thomas Jefferson (1743–1826), third president of the USA under the present constitution, was a Founding Father of the USA and a slave owner.

In the draft of this Declaration, Thomas Jefferson, a slave owner, had condemned the slave trade. However, it is clear that he believed that Africans were inferior beings to Europeans, and he was not prepared to give up his property or lose political influence through active opposition to slavery. The leaders of the American Revolution who were influenced by the ideas of the eighteenth-century Enlightenment were not social revolutionaries. When the federal constitution of the United States was drafted in 1787, the legal status of slavery in the Southern states, where about 90 per cent of American slaves lived, was strengthened.

In the 1790s, the French revolutionaries set out the principles of their revolution in a Declaration of the Rights of Man and of the Citizen that stated:

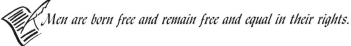 *Men are born free and remain free and equal in their rights.*

Despite the lofty ideals of the Enlightenment, political intrigue and economic self-interest meant that slavery and the slave trade would remain facts of life for too many people in the French empire. In 1794, the French abolished slavery in their colonies, and accepted all colonial males as full citizens, only for Napoleon Bonaparte to restore colonial slavery in 1802.

Humanitarian Ideals

Influenced by the ideals of the Enlightenment, some Europeans embarked on crusades against colonial slavery rather than against other forms of servitude and forced labour closer to home. From the beginning, campaigns against slavery exhibited a form of paternalism towards Africans and their descendants in European colonies. This approach was encouraged by real or imagined images of exotic, but apparently primitive, societies and cultures in Africa and the Americas, which gave some credibility to a simplistic moral crusade on behalf of Africans. Even those who opposed slavery were guilty of assuming that slaves were somehow inferior to free Europeans.

A public execution at Tyburn in London. A death sentence was common for most serious, as well as many less serious, crimes in eighteenth- and nineteenth-century Europe. How far did humanitarian ideals really extend at this time?

SLAVE LIFE IN THE AMERICAS

Slave Imports

More than 90 per cent of the slaves who were transported across the Atlantic were imported by European colonies on the South American mainland, or on the Caribbean islands. Conditions in these colonies were so harsh that slave deaths exceeded slave births. Climate, tropical diseases and exhausting labour on sugar plantations contributed to the failure of the slave populations in these ·colonies to achieve natural population growth. Slave owners continued to import large numbers of African slaves until the trade was abolished. Despite the existence of an illegal slave trade well into the nineteenth century, the slave population continued to decline.

The Sugar Trade

This illustration of sugar manufacture in the Antilles in 1726 is evidence of the labour-intensive production methods that were necessary to produce sugar that could be exported to Europe.

Several European states took advantage of the trading opportunities made possible by establishing colonies in the Americas. By the middle of the eighteenth century,

most European colonies in the region were committed to exporting sugar. Five British islands in the Caribbean produced cotton, timber, fish, livestock and salt, but fourteen British colonies concentrated on sugar production. By 1789, the French island of Saint-Domingue was the single largest sugar-producing colony in the Americas. The Dutch colony of Suriname on the mainland of South America imported African slaves to work on its plantations, and around one quarter of the population of the Danish island of Saint Thomas were slaves employed on sugar plantations. The Swedish colony of Saint Barthelemy was an exception in that its slaves were restricted to working as domestic servants or as farm labourers producing food for consumption on the island.

On sugar plantations, slaves worked under the gang system and were assigned tasks and roles according to colour of skin, place of birth, gender, state of health, age and skills. Slaves who were considered by their European owners to have lighter skins, and had been born in the Americas, were preferred for domestic service. Male and female slaves worked in the fields and there was little or no difference in the types of field work carried out by either sex. Men and women were expected to tackle the most arduous tasks in the fields and sugar factories. An eighteenth-century Swiss visitor to Saint-Domingue described how he saw,

Slaves planting sugar canes in Antigua in 1823. How would the working day of a plantation slave differ from the experience of a free labourer employed in similar activities?

about a hundred men and women of different ages, all occupied in digging ditches in a cane-field, the majority of them naked or covered in rags.

Field Labour on Plantations

At harvest time, slaves on sugar plantations had to work shifts of eighteen to twenty-four hours for five or six months at a time, since the sugar cane had to be processed without interruption. Field labour on sugar plantations was divided into three gangs. The first gang consisted of the fittest and healthiest slaves of both sexes who were experts in preparing the soil for cultivation, digging cane holes, planting and manuring the canes, burning and cutting the sugar cane at harvest time, and performing manual labour in the sugar mills. They worked under the supervision of European overseers and male slave-drivers.

The second gang was supervised by a male slave-driver and was made up of less fit males and females, pregnant or nursing females and slaves recently arrived from Africa. They performed a variety of less physically demanding tasks, including weeding crops, carrying manure to the cane fields and feeding crushed cane stalks into the sugar factory furnaces. The third gang consisted of children up to the age of twelve or thirteen who were supervised by a mature female slave, and this gang looked after the plantation's livestock.

Slaves employed in processing sugar cane developed considerable expertise and a range of skills that were valued by their owners. However, paying wages to an army of workers would have made these methods uneconomic.

On many Caribbean islands, and to a lesser extent in Brazil, a significant number of slaves were able to achieve a level of economic independence by cultivating crops on plots of land granted by their masters. These slaves could sell their surplus and acquire their own property and possessions.

Slave Emancipation

Despite attempts to bring the transatlantic slave trade to an end, African captives continued to be transported to the Americas for much of the nineteenth century, until slavery was abolished throughout South America and the Caribbean. A revolution in Saint-Domingue between 1791 and 1804 won independence for the French colony, and freed its slaves. The colony's slaves had marched to the words of a song that stated:

Better to die than go on being a slave.

Former slaves celebrating their emancipation in Barbados, August 1834. Similar scenes were repeated throughout the Americas in the nineteenth century by millions of freed labourers.

Sweden had handed back its only Caribbean colony to the French, long before slavery was abolished in the British Empire in 1834. All slaves were freed in the French and Danish colonies by 1848, and the Dutch abolished slavery in their colonies in 1863. Slavery came to an end in the Spanish Caribbean between 1870 and 1886, but Brazilian slaves were not emancipated until 1888.

Slavery remained profitable and therefore viable in both Brazil and Cuba until the 1870s, despite attempts by the Portuguese and Spanish governments to end the use of forced labour in both colonies. In the end, it would be political and technological change that would emancipate these slaves. In the case of Cuba, a more liberal regime in Spain and pro-independence rebels in the colony both declared their support for emancipation. Once the powerful plantation owners had built large, modern sugar mills, served by a network of railway lines, Cuban slaves were free to become wage labourers, employed on a seasonal basis. Direct action by free citizens, allied to the introduction of more efficient machinery in sugar mills, ended slavery in Brazil in the late 1880s.

As forced labour, most slaves employed in the fields had to be compelled to work by their owners and drivers. Beatings and whippings, or the threat of them, were a fact of life for most field hands.

Slavery in North America

Farmers in the North American colonies discovered that huge profits could be made from growing and exporting crops such as tobacco and cotton to Europe. Where fertile land was plentiful, but labour was in short supply, the most practical solution was the use of forced or slave labour. Some of the indigenous inhabitants of the colonies had been enslaved, but several factors prevented the development of large-scale slavery in this population, including the fact that so many of them had died in epidemics that swept through local communities with no immunity to diseases such as smallpox and measles. Also, the European colonists preferred to kill or drive away these people, rather than consider the employment of local inhabitants as agricultural labour.

From Indenture to Slavery

In the first half of the seventeenth century, the solution to the colonists' labour shortage was the employment of indentured or bond servants. Indentured servitude meant that Europeans unable to afford to pay for their own passage to the American colonies could sell their labour to colonists for an agreed number of years, in exchange for their transportation to America. Although criminals were transported to the American colonies, most bond servants were young males from poor backgrounds, attempting to escape from poverty, hunger, unemployment or military service. Children often served seven or more years, but most adults served four or five years of indentured service. Discipline could be brutal and the corporal punishment of runaways was a common practice.

From 1650 to 1700, although the free population of some colonies doubled or tripled, the number of indentured servants did not keep pace with the demand for farm labour. In Europe, higher wages and improved employment opportunities at home meant that fewer people were attracted to indentured servitude in North America. Colonial landowners who were unable to obtain a constant supply of European servants decided to use African slaves instead. Unlike indentured servitude, slavery was for life, and it was common for female slaves to pass their status on to their children, even if a child's father was a European. The African American writer W. E. B. DuBois wrote that:

 We cannot forget that America was built on Africa ... America became through African labour the centre of the sugar empire and the cotton kingdom.

American-born Slaves

Out of the ten to eleven million Africans who crossed the Atlantic on the Middle Passage, only six per cent of that total were taken to the British colonies in North America. In the eighteenth century, and in sharp contrast to the Caribbean and South America, the slave population of North America experienced a natural population growth. By the 1760s, the number of American-born slaves in the colonies overtook the number of African-born slaves. After the British ban on transatlantic slave-trading in 1807, the slave population of the United States of America more than tripled by 1860, from 1.2 million to 4 million, and only a tiny proportion of these slaves were African-born. The fact that so many slaves in North America had been born in the colonies meant that relations between free people and the slave population were profoundly different from those in the rest of the New World.

Slavery Declines in the North

Slaves had never formed a significant proportion of the population in the Northern colonies of the USA. Climate and soil conditions meant that plantation farming and the need for a large labour force did not develop in those colonies. In addition, religious and political principles in the Northern states meant that many people were uneasy at the existence of slavery in their communities. The growth of industry and urban communities in the North led to the development of a working class that was hostile to competition from slave labour. It was felt that slave labour would lead to lower wages and less favourable working conditions. As a result, anti-slavery campaigners found it relatively easy to rid the Northern states of slavery.

Slavery Develops in the South

The invention of Whitney's cotton gin, or engine, in the 1790s encouraged the rapid growth of cotton production in the Deep South of the USA. How different would the social and economic development of the Southern states have been without Whitney's invention?

Meanwhile, slavery had become entrenched in the South. The booming market in cotton was largely responsible for this development. To meet the growing demand for cotton fibre in British textile factories, plantation owners had needed to find a more efficient method of separating cotton seeds from their fibre. In the 1790s, Eli Whitney designed a machine that,

would clear the cotton with expedition (speed).

A horse-powered gin could seed fifty times as much cotton as before, in the same amount of time.

When cotton became the USA's main agricultural export in the first half of the nineteenth century, farmers discovered that large profits could be made from growing cotton on relatively small holdings, as well as larger plantations. This meant that most American slaves did not live on huge estates. In 1860, less than three per cent of slave owners in the South owned more than 50 slaves, and no more than one out of every thousand slave owners possessed more than 200 slaves. The larger plantations concentrated on growing sugar and rice. Cotton growers tended to live on their land, and personally supervised the work of their slaves. Only on larger plantations would professional overseers be employed to carry out the instructions of their employers, usually under the watchful eyes of a resident owner.

African slaves who worked on large Southern sugar plantations did so under the watchful eye of an overseer.

Life for Southern Slaves

The treatment and condition of slaves in the Southern states varied in relation to location, the crop grown, the size of farm or plantation and the attitude of the slave owner. On the other hand, it is possible to draw some general conclusions about slavery in the USA. Slavery was overwhelmingly based on agriculture. Most slaves were employed in the production of cotton, rice, tobacco, hemp, wheat, maize and sugar. Most lived on plantations and farms with between 15 and 50 slaves. Slaves had to endure a great deal. Malnutrition and disease were facts of life. Food, clothing and shelter were no more than basic for most slaves. Field hands worked hard, for little or no reward. Physical and sexual abuse were common.

Most non-capital offences against slaves escaped punishment or censure and only a few whites were tried, convicted and sentenced for murdering slaves. As well as beatings and mutilation for persistent runaways, the most effective deterrent to slave resistance was the constant threat of being sold and separated from family and friends, since no state's law recognised the existence or validity of slave marriages.

Slave Occupations

Slave occupations tended to be age-specific. Few able-bodied slaves aged fifteen to forty years of age were employed in occupations other than field work. Domestic servants tended to be older children, male and female, or older men and women no longer fit for heavy field work. Few slave owners could afford to have able-bodied slaves who specialised in a particular craft and worked full-time as carpenters or blacksmiths. Most urban slaves were female domestic servants, but some male slaves were employed as dock workers, craftsmen or factory workers employed in sugar processing or in sawmills.

Slaves were employed as house servants in the USA, as this eighteenth-century illustration shows. However, domestic service tended to be restricted to young slaves, or those too old or unfit to work in the fields.

Plantation Labour

On those plantations employing fifteen or more slaves, slaves would work in gangs led by a driver chosen from among the male slaves on account of his strength, intelligence, loyalty to his master and leadership skills. The driver acted as an assistant to the owner or overseer, and personally supervised the work of his slave gang. Slaves employed in field work tended to be described as either plough hands or hoe hands. Plough hands were the fittest, able-bodied male and female slaves. Hoe hands were less fit, but were regarded as being more important than the members of the trash gang. This third group was made up of adults incapable of heavy field work and young children, and they were employed in tasks such as weeding and yard cleaning. The gang system in the American South was very similar to organisation of gang labour on plantations in the Caribbean and South America (see page 28).

Domestic Life

Most slaves lived in wooden cabins or huts, and received a food allowance from their owners. It was common practice for field hands to receive four sets of clothes each year. Male field hands would be given trousers and a shirt, and women a dress. These clothes would have been sewn together by slave women, often using cloth that was specially manufactured in American textile

These log cabins were home to black field workers in Georgia, USA, in the 1860s.

mills to be sold to slave owners. Since boots and shoes seldom fitted properly, most field hands chose to work barefoot.

Many slaves were allowed to grow vegetables and keep chickens on small plots of land. Some were allowed to sell their produce at markets, or barter them for other goods. However, these garden plots were privileges that could be removed at the slave owner's discretion, and slaves were not able to pass on their property to their children or grandchildren.

Urban Slavery

The number of slaves employed in the towns and cities of the South was not significant. In the years immediately before the outbreak of the Civil War in 1861, slaves made up less than ten per cent of the population of the largest cities in the slave-owning states, and no more than five per cent of the population in smaller towns. Most owners were wary of allowing their slaves to associate with urban slaves, or the free African Americans who tended to live in urban areas rather than in rural regions. One abolitionist noted that,

 a city slave is almost a freeman, compared with a slave on a plantation.

Free African Americans

In the slave-owning states, most free African Americans lived in the upper South where more than ten per cent of all African Americans were free by 1810. Outside of that area, in the four decades before the outbreak of the Civil War, the number of free African Americans in the South decreased as states passed laws that made it very difficult for owners to free slaves. Free African Americans were encouraged to move north or west, despite the prejudice and discrimination they could face in those regions. In the Northern states, freedmen, as they were known, were denied a vote and legal protection, and were threatened by racist gangs or mobs.

About 30 per cent of the free African Americans living in the Southern states were described by their neighbours as 'people of colour'. Some were the descendants of unions between French or Spanish slaves and their owners, while others were refugees from the French colony of Saint-Domingue. These free people were called 'mulattoes' in official census documents, but some preferred to call themselves by the less offensive name of 'Creoles', which was a name also used by the European descendants of French and Spanish colonists. Some African American Creoles owned slaves. Another group of free 'coloureds' consisted of those freed slaves who were the sons and daughters of slave owners, whose parents had chosen to distinguish between them and their other slaves. This was a custom that was common in South America, but was much less common in the United States of America.

Christianity and Slavery

Some African captives were Christians before they arrived in the New World, but the widespread conversion of slaves to Christianity only began in the second half of the eighteenth century, and was accelerated by religious revivals among free Americans during the first half of the nineteenth century. In the last decades before emancipation, most slaves were Methodists or Baptists, like most of their Southern owners. In fact, a significant proportion of slaves attended the same services as their owners, although they worshipped in segregated slave galleries.

A religious revival in the USA at the beginning of the nineteenth century led to most slaves being converted to Christianity. This illustration from 1810 suggests that a slave's best hope of freedom would come from heaven … 'their day of grace has begun to dawn!'

Free African Americans had formed their own 'African' Baptist or Methodist churches in the late eighteenth century. In 1787, the Free African Society had been formed in Philadelphia by former slaves. Richard Allen, a freed slave, had founded the Bethel Church, and this grew into the African Methodist Episcopal Church in 1816. African churches were opened in the cities of the North, and in some urban areas of the South. African American communities, finding themselves excluded from so many organisations by prejudice and discrimination, went on to set up schools and other associations to serve their own communities.

Voodoo

At the same time, pre-Christian beliefs and practices persisted among rural slaves within their own families. Superstition, magic and folk remedies retained their hold on many illiterate farm labourers, and some slaves used potions, charms and rituals to ward off evil spirits, treat infections and frighten enemies. In southern Louisiana, the fusion of African beliefs and elements of Catholicism known as voodoo was popular, but it was virtually unknown in the rest of the South.

The Movement Towards Abolition

For most of the eighteenth century, few Europeans questioned the nature of the slave trade between Africa and the European colonies in the Americas, but towards the end of the century, an increasing number of people began to demand the abolition of the trade. The first Europeans to openly campaign against the slave trade were the Quakers, or Society of Friends, who declared in 1761 that no person engaged in the slave trade could be a member of their religion.

A significant move against the slave trade in the United Kingdom was made by Granville Sharp. He tried to use existing laws to fight against the trade. His most dramatic success concerned a runaway slave called Thomas Lewis who had been kidnapped by his former owner, and put on a ship bound for the West Indies. Sharp obtained permission to bring Lewis back to London, and for his case to be heard in court. The result was that a British court had to admit that it was not clear whether or not it was legal to possess a slave in the British Isles. In 1772, the case of James Somersett came to court. He was a slave who had lived as a free man in London for two years before being recaptured by his former owner. Sharp hired a team of lawyers who persuaded the judge, Lord Mansfield, that Somersett was a free man, and that it was illegal to force a runaway slave to leave the British Isles.

Granville Sharp (1735–1813) restraining a sea captain from taking a slave to his ship in 1767. Sharp was a founder of the British Society for the Abolition of the Slave Trade. He concentrated on fighting test cases through British courts to establish legal precedents that would force the trade to come to an end.

The *Zong*

In 1781, horrific events on the slave ship *Zong* focused public attention on the evils of the slave trade. The ship's captain was an experienced slave trader called Collingwood. He had mistaken Jamaica for Saint-Domingue, and after eleven weeks at sea, seven crew and over eighty slaves had died. In order to make a profit on the voyage, Collingwood ordered his crew to chain together and throw overboard more than 130 slaves so that he could make a claim to the ship's insurers. Ten slaves who witnessed what was happening committed suicide. Following a court case, the ship's owners were able to force the insurers to pay them £30 for each slave whom Collingwood had drowned.

The Campaign Begins

The Society for the Abolition of the Slave Trade was founded in 1787. The Society decided that its main purpose should be to campaign for an end to the transatlantic slave trade. The Society decided that the abolition of slavery would be too expensive if slave owners had to be compensated for the loss of their slaves, and the effects of the abolition of slavery on the colonies and transatlantic trade would hit the British economy too hard. Instead, by abolishing the slave trade they would end the wars in Africa that were fought to enslave thousands of Africans each year, bring to an end the horrors of the Middle Passage, and force slave owners to treat their slaves better, since they would be more difficult to replace.

Leading British abolitionists who campaigned for an end to the slave trade between the British Empire and Africa included Sharp, Macaulay, Wilberforce, Buxton and Clarkson.

Anti-Slave Trade Arguments

The Society claimed that sugar could be produced more cheaply in British-controlled India using free labour, or indentured servants, rather than by relying on slaves in the Americas. It argued that the transatlantic slave trade was holding back the development of British trade with India and the rest of Asia. The Society also produced evidence that hundreds of British seamen involved in the triangular trade died every year, and those who participated in the horrors of the Middle Passage were brutalised by the way that they were forced to treat their human cargoes. In 1798, a poet writing under the name 'Guineaman' described his experiences as a sailor on a slave ship with these words:

But some of them were sulky slaves,
And would not take their meat;
So therefore we were forced, by threats
And blows, to make them eat.

Gathering Evidence

Thomas Clarkson had been involved in setting up the Society in 1787 with Granville Sharp. Clarkson set himself the task of collecting evidence that would win support for the abolition of the slave trade. Embarking on his investigations in London, he visited and studied slave ships in the capital, as well as Bristol and Liverpool. He collected artefacts such as manacles, thumbscrews and branding irons. Despite intimidation and threats from slave ship captains and owners, Clarkson interviewed over 20,000 sailors and collected a mountain of evidence about the horrific conditions aboard slave ships. Much of this evidence was published, including detailed diagrams showing how slaves were stowed aboard the slave ships. First-hand evidence about the evils of the slave trade came from Olaudah Equiano who had been kidnapped in Africa as a child, but had been able to buy his freedom in the Caribbean. He later wrote about his experiences in *The Interesting Life of Olaudah Equiano*.

Kidnapped as a boy in Africa, Olaudah Equiano bought his freedom, became a leading abolitionist, and wrote his autobiography. He insisted on using his African name, rather than the slave name, Gustavus Vassa, given to him by his first owner.

William Wilberforce

William Wilberforce was a wealthy man whom John Newton, the former slave trader who had become a clergyman, had persuaded to join the Society for the Abolition of the Slave Trade. Wilberforce soon became its leader. In 1788, he wrote that:

> *The main object I have in view is the prevention of all further exports of slaves from Africa.*

Supported by evidence gathered by abolitionists that graphically illustrated the suffering of captives on the Middle Passage, Wilberforce worked hard to persuade Parliament to make it illegal to participate in the slave trade. However, the slave traders and slave-owning plantation owners had too many friends and allies among Members of Parliament, and Wilberforce's arguments failed to win the support of a majority of MPs.

As a consequence, the Society and its supporters stepped up their campaign for the abolition of the slave trade, and the abolitionists published even more horrific accounts of what happened on the Middle Passage and on plantations in British colonies. The pottery manufacturer, Josiah Wedgwood, produced china goods decorated with the Society's seal to publicise its campaign and raise funds for the abolitionist movement.

William Wilberforce (1759–1833) was thirty years of age when he began to campaign against the evils of the slave trade. As a Member of Parliament, he was able to put forward his arguments to the British government for the next eighteen years!

Slave Revolt in Saint-Domingue

Meanwhile, events in the Caribbean were taking a different turn. In 1789, the French people overthrew their king and in 1793 executed him. On the Caribbean island of Saint-Domingue, the slaves soon followed the revolutionary example of their French masters and, following a bloody revolt, they attempted to abolish plantation slavery. Saint-Domingue's slaves burned down plantations and slaughtered slave owners and their families. Ten thousand colonists fled to other colonies in the Caribbean and North America.

Jean-Baptiste Belley

In 1791, when the French National Assembly had decided to extend the Revolution's Declaration of the Rights of Man to include freed slaves and their descendants, but not slaves, French colonists had forced the government to back down. Three years later, a former Haitian slave from Saint-Domingue called Jean-Baptiste Belley, who was a deputy to the National Convention in Paris, made an impassioned speech that pledged Haitian loyalty to the cause of Revolution, but asked the Convention to abolish slavery. The Convention decreed that,

all men, without distinction of colour, domiciled in the colonies, are French citizens, and enjoy all the rights assured under the Constitution.

Belley demonstrated that African captives and their descendants could produce leaders of quality who could match their European counterparts in terms of eloquence and political skill.

Jean-Baptiste Belley was a former slave from Saint-Domingue who spoke at the National Convention in Paris on behalf of those of African descent who lived in France's Caribbean colonies.

A Growing Momentum

The liberation of Saint-Domingue (to be called Haiti) and the freeing of all its slaves had far-reaching consequences in the Americas and Europe. The slave revolutionaries forced the French revolutionaries to tackle the issues of racial equality and slave emancipation. The revolt removed France as a commercial rival to the British in the Caribbean, and contributed to the British decision to abolish their slave trade with Africa. Moreover, the example of the Haitians encouraged slave rebellions in other colonies. Later, the Haitians would provide assistance to General Simon Bolivar in his struggle against European colonisation in South America.

In 1791, a former slave called Francois-Dominique Toussaint Breda led the armed forces of the French colony of Saint-Domingue against British and Spanish invaders. Dropping the name Breda, he called himself 'L'Ouverture' (French for 'opening'), and in 1801 he declared that the colony was an independent state.

The British Relent

Back in Britain, every year for nearly two decades, Wilberforce tried, but failed, to persuade the British Parliament to abolish the slave trade. But in 1807, both Houses of Parliament voted to pass a law abolishing the slave trade between Britain, Africa and all British colonies. British traders and ships could no longer participate in the transatlantic slave trade. In fact, the Royal Navy would try to prohibit other countries' ships from trading in slaves.

In all, 283 British Members of Parliament had voted for the abolition of the slave trade, and only sixteen voted against. Despite Wilberforce and his fellow abolitionists having fought against the slave trade for more than thirty years, in the end, political and economic circumstances persuaded their opponents to accept that abolition was in British interests.

The British naval victory at Trafalgar in 1805 had ended the threat from the French and Spanish navies, and the British wanted to take full advantage of their sea power. They could stop and search foreign vessels, using the pretext of halting the transatlantic slave trade, to deprive the French, Spanish, Portuguese and Dutch colonies, as well as the American states, of new batches of African captives. In the process, they were able to disrupt enemy trade. This took place at a time when British prosperity no longer relied on slave labour in the colonies since domestic industries had developed rapidly. British plantation owners in the Caribbean were also keen to make life difficult for their rivals by ending the trade.

British naval supremacy was confirmed at the Battle of Trafalgar, and paved the way for British efforts to bring the transatlantic slave trade to an end, from 1807.

British Opposition to Abolition

There were many reasons why it had taken so long to persuade Britain's political leaders to abolish the transatlantic trade in African captives. One reason was that the slave trade had many powerful supporters. Plantation owners based in the Caribbean, the merchants who bought their produce, and the absentee plantation owners living in Britain, some of them Members of Parliament, were well organised as well as powerful. They had enough wealth to bribe other Members of Parliament to support them. They also had the support of King George III until he became too ill to influence government policy. Many influential people were prepared to believe that the abolitionists had exaggerated the number of occasions when slaves had been badly treated. They believed that the enterprise of slave-owning planters had helped to make Britain wealthy and prosperous.

Wars Against France

Another factor that delayed the abolition of the slave trade was the French Revolutionary Wars. Britain had joined an alliance of countries that had gone to war against the new republican government of France. This conflict did not end until 1815, when Napoleon was defeated at the Battle of Waterloo. These wars made heavy financial demands on Britain, and most politicians believed that ending the slave trade would be too costly. It was also claimed that the transatlantic trade was an essential training ground for the Royal Navy that defended the British Isles from invasion.

Napoleon (1769–1821), Emperor of France, embarked on a series of wars of conquest against other European states. These wars had repercussions for European colonies in the Caribbean, as well as North and South America.

The Effects of British Abolition in the USA

Agriculture in the American South relied on slave labour. Once the British began to bring the legal trade in African captives to an end, slave trading between states grew in scale and profitability. As plantation farming in the upper South declined in states such as Maryland, Virginia, North Carolina and South Carolina, demand for slaves grew in states where cotton plantations were making large profits. As the *Charleston Mercury* noted before the Civil War:

Slaves are as much and as frequently articles of commerce as the sugar and molasses which they produce.

Slave traders were everywhere in the South. Some companies had branch offices in towns and cities throughout the slave states. They advertised in newspapers, offering high prices for fit and healthy slaves, and visited farms and plantations to offer owners cash for slaves who would fetch good prices at auction. New Orleans was the largest slave-trading centre in the Deep South, handling slaves from the upper South being sold to the thriving cotton and sugar growing areas.

The internal slave trade within the USA led to untold suffering within the African American community. In the decades before the Civil War, as slave traders sought to maintain profit margins, it was common for families to be split up as individuals were sold to the highest bidder. It was not unusual for husbands to be sold separately from their wives, and for parents to be separated from their children. A former slave, Josiah Henson, described how as a young child:

The inhumanity of slave ownership and the trade in human beings is illustrated by this poster. It lists people for sale, giving their age, physical attributes, and details of any skills or training that will increase their value to a potential purchaser.

My brothers and sisters were bid off first, one by one, while my mother, paralysed by grief, held me by the hand.

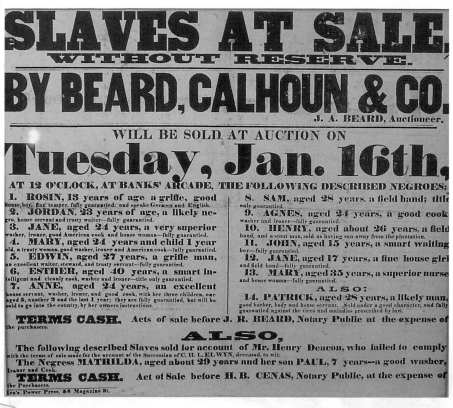

SLAVES AT SALE,
WITHOUT RESERVE.
BY BEARD, CALHOUN & CO.
J. A. BEARD, Auctioneer.

WILL BE SOLD AT AUCTION ON

Tuesday, Jan. 16th,

AT 12 O'CLOCK, AT BANKS' ARCADE, THE FOLLOWING DESCRIBED NEGROES:

1. **ROSIN, 13** years of age a griffe, good house boy, fine temper, fully guarantied, and speaks German and English.
2. **JORDAN, 23** years of age, a likely negro, house servant and trusty waiter—fully guarantied.
3. **JANE, aged 24** years, a very superior washer, ironer, good American cook and house woman—fully guarantied.
4. **MARY, aged 24** years and child 1 year old, a trusty woman, good washer, ironer and American cook—fully guarantied.
5. **EDWIN, aged 27** years, a griffe man, an excellent waiter, steward, and trusty servant—fully guarantied.
6. **ESTHER, aged 40** years, a smart intelligent and cleanly cook, washer and ironer—title only guarantied.
7. **ANNE, aged 24** years, an excellent house servant, washer, ironer, and good cook, with her three children, one aged 5, another 3 and the last 1 year; they are fully guarantied, but will be sold to go into the country, by her owners instructions.

8. **SAM, aged 28** years, a field hand; title only guarantied.
9. **AGNES, aged 24** years, a good cook washer and ironer—fully guarantied.
10. **HENRY, aged about 26** years, a field hand, and a stout man, sold as having ran away from the plantation.
11. **JOHN, aged 15** years, a smart waiting boy—fully guarantied.
12. **JANE, aged 17** years, a fine house girl and field hand—fully guarantied.
13. **MARY, aged 35** years, a superior nurse and house woman—fully guarantied.

ALSO:

14. **PATRICK, aged 28** years, a likely man, good barber, body and house servant. Sold under a good character, and fully guarantied against the vices and maladies prescribed by law.

TERMS CASH. Acts of sale before J. R. BEARD, Notary Public at the expense of the purchasers.

ALSO,

The following described Slaves sold for account of Mr. Henry Deacon, who failed to comply with the terms of sale made for the account of the Succession of C. H. L. ELWYN, deceased, to wit:

The Negress **MATHILDA**, aged about 29 years and her son **PAUL, 7** years—a good washer, Ironer and Cook.

TERMS CASH. Act of Sale before H. B. CENAS, Notary Public, at the expense of the Purchasers.

...n's Power Press, 58 Magazine St.

THE ABOLITION OF SLAVERY IN THE USA

Revolts and Sabotage

The most common form of resistance to slavery was called 'silent sabotage'. Many slaves expressed their discontent by vandalising owners' property, and stealing food and other objects from the masters and their families. Whenever possible, gangs of field hands opposed efforts to impose a strict routine on their working day. The result was that most gangs tended to work long hours at a leisurely pace, interrupted by short periods of intense activity, often carried out under the threat of the master's whip. Few field hands were forced to work on Sundays, and some owners felt obliged to pay their slaves to work on the Sabbath at harvest time.

The most extreme form of resistance to the institution of slavery in the South was confrontation. Slaves would offer physical resistance to whites in extreme circumstances, such as when they were provoked by violent or abusive slave owners or overseers, or threatened by the sale of a family member to another estate some distance away. The few major slave revolts that erupted were local affairs, and they were swiftly crushed by the use of armed force. The most bloody slave revolt in American history took place in 1811, when 500 slaves in Louisiana marched on New Orleans, led by a former slave-driver called Charles Deslondes. More than 60 slaves were killed in battle or executed in the aftermath of the rebellion. The most famous slave-led insurrection was Nat Turner's revolt in Southampton County, Virginia, in 1831. Turner held out for two months, until he was captured, tried and executed.

Runaways

Most successful runaways were young adult males from the states of Maryland, Virginia, Kentucky and Missouri, fortunate in having less distance to travel to reach the free states in the North. Most fugitive slaves hid out close to their owners' plantations. Some eluded capture long enough to join the free African American

Many people risked their lives and freedom to assist runaway slaves to escape from their owners.

The fact that rewards were offered for the return of runaways suggests that people had to be encouraged to capture slaves who were fleeing from their masters.

population in the larger towns, but most runaways were captured.

Some runaways received food and shelter from sympathetic people whom they met on their journey, and others were guided by around 3,000 'conductors' on the so-called 'Underground Railroad' who broke the law to assist runaways. It has been estimated that possibly 75,000 slaves escaped to freedom using this network of routes north from the slave states. The fugitive slave, Harriet Tubman, is credited with having conducted at least 300 runaways to freedom, including escorting a group of eleven fugitives to freedom in Canada.

Maroon Communities

A small number of escaped slaves formed groups of fugitives known as 'maroons' living in inaccessible swamps in Florida, remote sea islands in South Carolina, and unsettled areas of Georgia. Sometimes, the maroons would undertake expeditions to attack plantations and take slaves back with them to enlarge their communities. Persistent truants could expect to be brutally beaten or maimed, but even runaways who simply took off to visit friends or relatives, or escape censure for some minor misdemeanour, would be fortunate to receive no more than verbal abuse from their owners.

$00,00 REWARD!

RANAWAY from the subscriber, on the 10th inst., a Negro Man named Jack, about 35 years of age, about 5 feet 5 inches high, weighs 125 or 130 lbs., dark copper color, some teeth out before, has an impediment in his walk as if he were stiff in the hip joint, his clothing consisted of black cloth pantaloons, blue cloth close bodied coat, and black over coat, boots and over shoes--boots have been lately half-soled;--also a black oil cloth satchel. I will give $25 if taken in the county, $50 if taken out of the county, or $100 if taken out of the State, or lodged in any jail that I may get him, or delivered to me in Haynesville, Clinton County, Missouri.
TAYLOR HULEN.

March 12, 1858.

Early American Abolitionists

In the early years of the American republic, anti-slavery ideals were popular in Northern and Southern states. Many recognised the conflict between the ideals of the republic's constitution and the harsh realities of slave life. Slavery did not sit well with liberal, humanitarian beliefs, and many Americans had been influenced by the radical social and political ideas that came out of Revolutionary France. Other Americans recognised the conflict between slave ownership and Christian beliefs. This period saw a rapid and irreversible decline in the number of slaves in the Northern states.

By the early nineteenth century, the rapid economic development of Southern agriculture and the fact that plantation production exploited large numbers of slave labourers appeared to push anti-slavery organisations into the background. A key figure in reviving the anti-slavery movement was William Lloyd Garrison who founded the anti-slavery newspaper *The Liberator* in 1831. In 1833, the American Anti-Slavery Society was founded, demanding immediate emancipation without compensation to slave owners. Within a few years, membership of the Society's 1,500 branches was believed to stand at 250,000 in the Northern states.

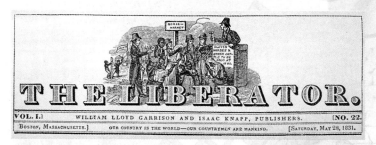

The masthead of William Lloyd Garrison's abolitionist newspaper, *The Liberator*, 1831. This newspaper published stories of successful runaways and provided details of slave owners' abuses of their slaves.

Frederick Douglass, a runaway slave who became an agent for the Anti-Slavery Society, travelled widely in the North, lecturing against slavery and campaigning for the rights of free African Americans. He published the first of three autobiographies, *The Narrative of the Life of Frederick Douglass: An American Slave* in 1845. To escape recapture, he sailed to Britain, and in 1846 British friends purchased his freedom from Hugh Auld, his former owner.

Many people in the North were abolitionists because they believed that slavery was cruel and inhuman. Some opposed slavery because of the harm that it did to whites in slave-owning areas. They believed that it encouraged cruelty to other humans by brutalising owners and overseers, while poor whites who did not own land or slaves found it difficult to find work, and became lazy or turned to crime.

Harriet Beecher Stowe's novel appealed to hundreds of thousands of Americans in the free states who sympathised with the plight of the novel's African American hero.

Uncle Tom's Cabin

In March 1852, Harriet Beecher Stowe published her novel, *Uncle Tom's Cabin*. She based this work on stories of runaway slaves, and set out to persuade her readers that the evils of slavery had to be ended immediately. Around 100,000 copies of the book were purchased in its first week of publication, and more than two million copies were bought within two years. Other anti-slavery novels had been published before, including Richard Hildreth's *The Slave, or the Memoirs of Archy Moore* in 1836, but *Uncle Tom's Cabin* tapped into a new mood. Mary Chesnut, the wife of a plantation owner, complained in her diary in 1862 that:

People (in the North) expect more virtue from a plantation African than they can find in practice among themselves.

Emancipation Plans

Some Northerners feared the results of emancipating slaves while others opposed granting freed African Americans political equality. Consequently, some Northerners supported the idea of setting up colonies of former slaves in either Central America or West Africa, rather than encouraging former slaves to become citizens of the USA. Most Northerners opposed the spread of slavery into the Western territories, and this increased political tensions between free and slave states.

This illustration, dating from 1852, shows one of the novel's characters, George, handing out certificates of freedom to his slaves. Note how the artist has chosen to portray the slaves' reaction to this news in a most undignified light.

Sectionalism

Southerners feared that the North would try to forbid slavery in the West, and both 'sections' became concerned at the possibility of a shift in the balance of power between North and South that would mean either the slave or free states would be in the majority. The Missouri Compromise of 1820 had balanced the number of slave-owning and free states, and this had limited discussion about the spread of slavery into the West for a generation.

The 1850 Compromise was supposed to solve the problem of allowing California to enter the Union by allowing it to become a free state, so long as stricter laws were passed to make it easier to return escaped slaves to their owners. The Kansas–Nebraska Act of 1854 tried to allow both states to join the Union, so long as both held a referendum to decide whether either would be a slave-owning or a free state. This attempt to find a compromise led to violence and bloodshed.

Tensions between free and slave states grew, and in 1857 the decision of the Supreme Court in the Dred Scott Case concerning the ownership of a runaway slave appeared to extend the rights of slave owners into the free states. In 1859, the abolitionist John Brown tried to initiate a slave revolt in Virginia, and the whole issue of slavery and states' rights went on to dominate the presidential election of the following year.

John Brown's attempt at a slave revolt ended in failure. Here, Union soldiers are bringing Brown's followers out of the engine house at Harpers Ferry.

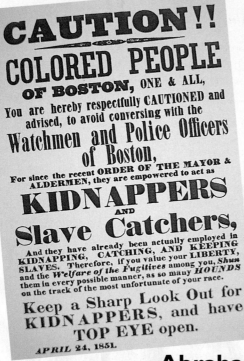

CAUTION!!
COLORED PEOPLE
OF BOSTON, ONE & ALL,
You are hereby respectfully CAUTIONED and advised, to avoid conversing with the
Watchmen and Police Officers
of Boston,
For since the recent ORDER OF THE MAYOR & ALDERMEN, they are empowered to act as
KIDNAPPERS
AND
Slave Catchers,
And they have already been actually employed in KIDNAPPING, CATCHING, AND KEEPING SLAVES. Therefore, if you value your LIBERTY, and the Welfare of the Fugitives among you, Shun them in every possible manner, as so many HOUNDS on the track of the most unfortunate of your race.

Keep a Sharp Look Out for **KIDNAPPERS**, and have **TOP EYE** open.

APRIL 24, 1851.

This poster of 1851 illustrates some of the national tensions. It warns fugitive slaves to stay away from watchmen and police officers in the Boston area who were acting as kidnappers and slave catchers.

National Tensions

By 1860, national politics in the USA were sectional, and politicians and parties reflected the widening gap between North and South over the issue of slave-holding in the Western territories. Issues that resulted from territorial expansion and economic growth, such as the further development of the railroads, were viewed from the perspective of both sections. Increasingly, many Northerners believed that there was a slave power conspiracy that influenced the actions of the executive and decisions taken by the courts. Many Southerners were convinced that the institution of slavery could be preserved only by secession from the Union.

Abraham Lincoln

When the Republican candidate, Abraham Lincoln, was elected President of the USA in 1860, many Southerners were convinced that he would try to abolish slavery. Starting with South Carolina, Southern states voted to secede from the Union. In March 1861, the Vice President of their newly-formed Confederacy said that,

our Confederacy is founded upon ... the great truth that the black is not equal to the white man. That slavery, subordination to the superior race, is his natural and normal condition.

Lincoln believed that slavery was morally wrong and against the spirit, if not the letter, of the Declaration of Independence and the other ideals of the Founding Fathers. He opposed the expansion of slavery into the Western territories, but he was not an abolitionist at that time. In 1861, he said,

I have no purpose, directly or indirectly, to interfere with the institution of slavery.

Following his election victory, Lincoln was not convinced that the secessionists in the South would carry out their threat to divide the Union, but he was careful not to say or do anything that would heighten the crisis.

Abraham Lincoln (1809–65), US President, 1860–65.

The Civil War

Lincoln was not prepared to allow the Southern states to set up a separate Confederacy. The President's primary war aim would be to preserve the Union, not to abolish slavery. As late as August 1862, the President wrote,

What I do about slavery, and the coloured race, I do because I believe it helps to save the Union ...

The war aims of the Confederacy were to preserve slavery, and to fight a defensive war against invasion from the North. As the war progressed, the South hoped to force the North into negotiating a truce that would recognise Southern independence. To this end, the Confederates hoped to enlist support from the United Kingdom and France. To achieve these aims, the Confederates had to defeat the Union forces in the East, the West and at sea.

In the East, the fighting centred on Northern Virginia, the Shenandoah Valley, Maryland and Pennsylvania. In the West, the fighting took place in Tennessee, Georgia and along the Mississippi River. The war at sea focused on Union attempts to blockade Confederate ports and restrict Southern trade with other countries, and Confederate attempts to prevent the Union forces combining their military forces to capture ports and fortresses on important rivers. The first major battle of the war took place at Bull Run near Washington DC, in July 1861.

A contemporary illustration of the battle of Bull Run in July 1861. People in the Northern states took a keen interest in news of the campaigns and battles of the Civil War, often taking place hundreds of miles to the south and east.

War and Freedom

From the beginning of the war, Lincoln's generals had to deal with those slaves freed by advancing Union forces. In 1861, General Butler, who commanded a Union army base in Virginia, declared that three fugitive slaves who had escaped from a Confederate labour battalion were enemy property liable to be seized, or 'contraband of war'. He gave them food, shelter and work and, within two months, there were about 1,000 contrabands at his base. Later in the same year, General Fremont, who commanded the Union forces in Missouri, issued a proclamation declaring that the slaves of every rebel in the state were free.

Emancipation Proclamation

In September 1861, Lincoln modified Fremont's proclamation so that it freed only those slaves used directly in the Confederate war effort. However, it was not long before Lincoln recognised the strategic value of emancipating all slaves in enemy territory. In 1863, Lincoln's Emancipation Proclamation meant that the abolition of slavery had become one of his government's war aims. As commander in chief, the President declared that all slaves in rebel territory were,

thenceforward, and forever free.

The Proclamation did not free any slaves, since slaves living in the four slave states loyal to the Union, and in Confederate territory captured by the Union armies, were not included in the terms of the document. What the Proclamation made clear was that the North was fighting for a Union freed from the moral burden of slavery.

Emancipated slaves travelling north following Lincoln's proclamation in 1863. This fictional scene exaggerates the number of freed men and women who headed north from Confederate territory to the free states.

W. T. Sherman (1820–91), general of the Union army in Georgia and South Carolina, 1864–65, in heroic pose.

On The Road to Emancipation

At the end of 1864, General Sherman issued Special Field Order Number 15, granting the Carolina Sea Islands and all of the fertile plantation land 48km inland, from Charleston to Jacksonville, to freed slaves. General Saxton who commanded the Union occupation forces settled more than 40,000 freed slaves on this land until Lincoln's successor, President Johnson, pardoned the rebel landowners and returned their property to them.

Despite the success of the Union campaign after 1863, most slaves were not emancipated until the Confederacy had been defeated. Although more than 500,000 contrabands escaped to freedom behind Union lines, more than three million slaves continued to work on Southern farms and plantations throughout the Civil War. The Confederate war department drafted thousands of slaves to work as labourers for the army, and many other slaves accompanied their masters to war as servants. However, many slaves gave food, shelter and other aid to Union prisoners of war trying to escape from Confederate custody. As well as working as free labourers, contrabands assisted Union troops by supplying them with local intelligence, and the absence of owners and overseers serving in the Confederate armed forces reduced the contribution of slave labour to the Southern economy.

In January 1865, the Thirteenth Amendment to the US Constitution was passed, abolishing slavery in every state of the Union, and emancipating nearly four million African Americans. Within four years, the Fourteenth and Fifteenth Amendments and the Civil Rights Act of 1866 confirmed the voting rights and civil rights of the freed slaves.

A Union victory parade held in Washington DC on 23 May 1865. The victorious North celebrated the defeat of the Confederacy, rather than the emancipation of the slaves.

Reasons for Union Victory

The Union's superior economic resources contributed to the defeat of the Confederacy. Another factor was the collapse of the Confederate forces' supply system, and the subsequent weakening of Southern morale in the face of Union advances. This led to a flood of desertions from the Southern armies in the later stages of the war. In addition, President Lincoln had a firm grasp of strategy and knew that defeating the Confederate army was more important than occupying enemy territory. To achieve this end, he takes full credit for appointing Ulysses S. Grant to command his armies in 1864. In sharp contrast, Jefferson Davis as Confederate leader failed to convince the Southern people that he could lead them to victory.

The Contribution of African Americans

The contribution of African Americans to the Union war effort had made possible the defeat of the Confederacy. Ten thousand African Americans served in the Union navy from the outbreak of the war. At the end of 1862, Lincoln authorised the enlistment of freed slaves into the Union army. More than 190,000 African Americans served in the Union armed forces. They made up nearly ten per cent of enlisted men, they received equal pay from 1864 onwards and, despite racial prejudice, nearly 100 African Americans were commissioned in the army. Seventeen African American soldiers and four sailors received Congressional Medals of Honour. The rebels did not authorise the enlistment of slaves into the Confederate army until March 1865, and they had surrendered before a regiment of slave troops could be established.

A proud soldier who had escaped from slavery to join the Union army. This illustration appeared in *Harper's Weekly* magazine in 1864.

African American Culture

The ending of the legal slave trade with Africa and the rest of the New World led to a decline in the influence of African culture on American slaves after 1800. Instead, their shared, common experiences as enslaved rural labourers became important. The movement of slaves within the USA due to the domestic slave trade that developed when the slave trade with Africa ended, also helped to create a common culture among slaves in the South.

Elaborate slave marriage and funeral ceremonies were used to mark key stages in human existence. Slave children grew up listening to similar fables and folk tales told throughout the South. Great respect was accorded to the preachers, folk doctors, midwives, musicians and storytellers who served the African American slave community, and who helped to develop a distinct African American identity before the outbreak of the Civil War.

Measured in thousands rather than millions, some freed slaves marked their emancipation by moving west, constructing railroads, working on cattle ranches and claiming their own homesteads on the Great Plains. It was not until the twentieth century that millions of African Americans abandoned their rural traditions and headed north to live in an urban environment.

The defeat of the slave states in the Civil War opened the way for the westward expansion of the railroad network. Some African Americans took the opportunity to move west, but the main feature of this development was the destruction of the tribes who lived on the Great Plains.

Sojourner Truth (c.1797–1883), a former slave who became a Christian preacher and abolitionist. Like so many African American abolitionists, her work was overlooked by historians until the second half of the twentieth century.

Frederick Douglass (c.1818–95) became such a famous runaway abolitionist that a song was composed in his honour by Jesse Hutchinson in 1845.

African American Abolitionists

In the decades before emancipation, some of the most effective spokespersons for the abolitionists were runaway or former slaves, such as Frederick Douglass, J. W. Loguen, Sojourner Truth, William W. Brown and Henry H. Garnet. In 1843, Garnet announced to the Convention of Free People of Colour, in New York:

Remember that you are four millions! Let your motto be resistance, resistance, RESISTANCE!

African American abolitionists wanted to shape their own destiny. They had no desire to be the beneficiaries of the paternalism of their abolitionist allies, such as William Lloyd Garrison and John Brown. Frederick Douglass tried, but failed, to persuade John Brown not to attempt his raid on Harpers Ferry in 1859.

The Black Codes

In the American South, the original Black Codes had been introduced as early as 1680 to prevent slave rebellions, but these laws had been developed to control every aspect of slave life. Plantation owners, their overseers, their friends and relatives, as well as local townspeople and police, served in patrols set up to enforce the codes in their area. Plantation owners usually paid for the patrols, and failure to serve in one led to a fine. Each patrol was mounted on horseback, armed and accompanied by dogs, and headed by a captain. The patrols could seize and punish any slaves whom they considered to be absent from their plantations without permission, or guilty of breaking the local curfew for African Americans. Slaves who tried to resist the patrol could be shot, and patrols could enter slave cabins to search for weapons, or simply to intimidate the African American community. After emancipation, it was easy for racists to adopt the patrol model and use it as an effective method of shutting off African Americans from most avenues of freedom and self-expression.

THE EFFECTS OF ABOLITION ON AFRICA

Seeking Alternatives

British sailors chasing a slave trader's dhow, or yacht, near Zanzibar in East Africa. European states tried to bring the African slave trade to an end during the second half of the nineteenth century.

The long-standing trade in slaves across the Saharan region did not increase sufficiently to replace the export of slaves across the Atlantic. Attempts to preserve the transatlantic slave trade meant dealing with illegal traders who were often unable or unwilling to guarantee steady profits for African merchants. In comparison to the trade in captives, the total value of exports of palm oil, timber, gold and other products to Europe and the Americas was small. Some West African states had developed their own plantation agriculture, using slaves to produce rice, coffee and cotton. A significant success was the spread of peanut or groundnut cultivation for export, from the Senegal River region to Sierra Leone. Another positive development was the growth of the cocoa industry on the West African Gold Coast from the 1860s.

However, within forty years, small trading stations had become huge European colonies that incorporated former independent African states. Sierra Leone and Liberia became colonies for small communities of former slaves. Around 13,000 African Americans had settled in Liberia by 1867. By the end of the nineteenth century, the British colony of Sierra Leone controlled around 43,000 square kilometres of territory, and the British colony on the Gold Coast expanded to take control of the Ashanti Confederation and extensive 'Northern Territories'. Within forty years, the tiny British colony of Lagos had grown to include most of present-day Nigeria, the second largest state in Africa today. The West African colonies of other European states grew in a similar fashion during this period.

European Paternalism in Africa

The modern map of Africa, with its regular boundaries drawn along lines of latitude and longitude, bears little or no relation to the boundaries of ancient kingdoms and empires. Instead, it is a product of nineteenth-century European aggression. Many Europeans perceived the failure of so many African economies to find alternatives to the slave trade as a clear sign that Africans were somehow less advanced than themselves. The long and brutal history of African servitude in the Americas had encouraged many Europeans to adopt a paternalistic attitude towards Africa that justified its subjugation and colonisation, so long as it was accompanied by the expansion of Christian missionary activities.

A map of Africa pre-1914, showing the imperial acquisitions of European states.

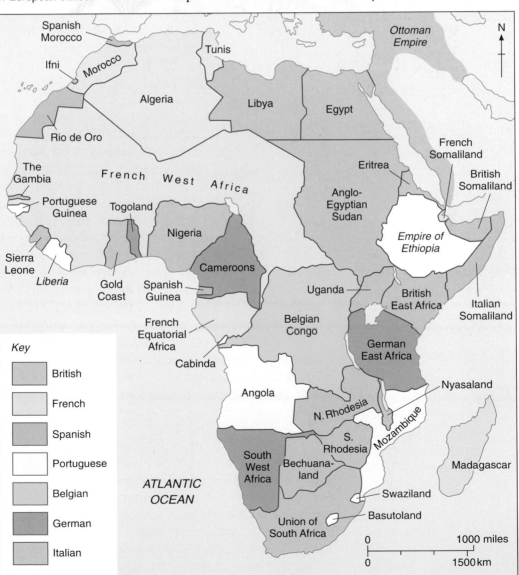

Key

- British
- French
- Spanish
- Portuguese
- Belgian
- German
- Italian

Spanish Morocco, Ifni, Morocco, Tunis, Ottoman Empire, Algeria, Libya, Egypt, Rio de Oro, The Gambia, French West Africa, Eritrea, French Somaliland, British Somaliland, Portuguese Guinea, Togoland, Nigeria, Anglo-Egyptian Sudan, Empire of Ethiopia, Sierra Leone, Liberia, Gold Coast, Spanish Guinea, Cameroons, Uganda, British East Africa, Italian Somaliland, French Equatorial Africa, Belgian Congo, Cabinda, German East Africa, Angola, Nyasaland, N. Rhodesia, Mozambique, S. Rhodesia, South West Africa, Bechuanaland, Madagascar, ATLANTIC OCEAN, Swaziland, Union of South Africa, Basutoland

0   1000 miles
0   1500km

This attack on Dahomey, a coastal region of West Africa, by French troops in 1892 involved the murder of a large number of Africans. Africans were no longer needed as captives, but those who survived these attacks were to become subjects of European states.

The 'Scramble for Africa'

The destruction of independent African states in West Africa in the decades following the European withdrawal from the slave trade, was repeated in the European conquest of North, South and East Africa in the same period. African resistance provoked brutal reprisals to safeguard European colonists. In the second half of the nineteenth century, African resistance to European aggression provoked further European conquest. Several European states expanded existing colonies, founded new colonies, or established protectorates where land was not occupied by the European state, but the territory was recognised as being in that state's sphere of influence.

European Rivalry

In Europe, participation in what became known as the 'Scramble for Africa' was regarded as a defensive act. Europeans states believed that their African colonies had to be protected from economic competition from the colonies or protectorates of other European states, as well as attacks from local Africans and their rulers. At that time, there were intense political and economic rivalries between European states that made them keen to acquire new African colonies and extend existing colonies, often simply to prevent territory falling into the hands of rivals. One British politician wrote in 1892:

 We are to effect the reconquest of Equatoria and occupy the Albert Lakes and the whole basin of the Upper Nile. Why? For fear of the French, the Germans, the Belgians etc, etc.

Technological developments in nineteenth-century Europe meant that African armies could do little more than delay the advance of European armies into the interior of the continent. Europeans tried to temper this aggression by claiming that they were striving to wipe out African slavery, and Africa's slave trade with Asia.

European Colonies in Africa

The British, long established in Cape Colony on the southern tip of Africa, extended their colonies in West Africa, seized territory in East Africa, gained control over Egypt, which had been under Ottoman Turkish rule, and with Egypt dominated Sudan. The French took over most of West and Equatorial Africa, and Madagascar in East Africa. The Portuguese established their control over Angola and Mozambique while Spain ruled the northern part of Morocco and the area of Western Sahara. Germany took territory in South-West Africa and East Africa, now known as Namibia and Tanzania, and Italy established colonies in what are now Libya, Eritrea and Somalia. An African poet in Ghana wrote in 1900:

'We've come to trade!!' they said,
'To reform the beliefs of the people,
To halt oppression here below, and theft,
To clean up and overthrow corruption',
Not all of us grasped their motives,
So now we've become their inferiors.

Tippu Tib, a powerful African slave trader in the 1880s, grew very wealthy from the sale of captives and ivory to other traders. Tippu Tib's lands were conquered by a Belgian army, and made part of the Congo Free State.

Rubber Terror

King Leopold II of Belgium personally controlled the Congo Free State from 1885 to 1908, a vast territory that was bigger than the United Kingdom, France, Germany, Spain and Italy combined. In this protectorate, all suitable land was divided between concession companies. In rubber-growing areas, forced labour, hostage-taking, brutal beatings, chain gangs and the destruction of whole villages were employed to subdue and control the African population. These atrocities, committed in the name of the ruler of a small European state, highlight how far the balance of power in Africa had shifted in favour of European colonists.

Similar forced labour systems for extracting rubber were in place in the French territories west and north of the Congo River, in Portuguese-ruled Angola, and in German-controlled Cameroon. African refugees who fled across the Congo River to escape Leopold's ruthless regime often fled back to escape the French brutality in Congo-Brazzaville, and the population loss in this region was nearly 50 per cent within twenty years. The 'rubber terror' was one of the most barbaric episodes in the European colonisation of Africa.

The rule of Leopold II over his personal empire in Africa, was one of the most brutal and bloodthirsty episodes in the modern history of Africa.

UP FROM SLAVERY

American Reconstruction

When the American Civil War ended in 1865, around four million American slaves had been emancipated. For the next few years, national politics in the USA were dominated by discussions on the nature and extent of the reconstruction programme that would be directed at the former slave states. This was done without the leadership and guidance of Abraham Lincoln, who had been assassinated at the end of the war.

Legislation passed and ratified by Congress between 1865 and 1870 granted equal civil and political rights to all African Americans. The Civil Rights Act of 1866 defined all persons born in the United States as American citizens with equal rights. The Fourteenth Amendment to the constitution ratified in 1868 incorporated the Civil Rights Act's definition of citizenship into the constitution, and the Fifteenth Amendment ratified in 1870 declared that,

President Ulysses S. Grant (1822–85), signed the Fifteenth Amendment to the US constitution in March 1870. African Americans soon discovered that laws and constitutional amendments did not guarantee civil rights in a racist community.

the right of citizens of the United States to vote shall not be denied or abridged by the United States or by any State on account of race, colour, or previous condition of servitude.

However, in line with the views of most Americans, there would be no major social welfare programme to assist freed slaves. As the abolitionist Frederick Douglass had said in 1862,

the best way to help them is just to let them help themselves.

Instead, the Freedmen's Bureau was established in May 1865, to distribute food to refugees and the destitute of every race, provide limited health care, establish free labour farming, and assist in the establishment of schools for the children of former slaves. The Bureau's affairs were wound up in 1872.

Sharecropping

Racial prejudices in the South forced the authorities to establish separate facilities for former slaves and their children, often providing inferior services to African Americans. Having freed the slaves without compensating their former owners, the federal government was not willing to go further and confiscate the owners' plantations and redistribute the land to former slaves. However, governments in the South sought to establish a free labour economy, and former slaves celebrated their freedom by refusing to work for overseers or under the gang labour system. As a result, the plantation system of production soon disappeared. Many female former slaves marked their freedom by abandoning fieldwork, and many families opted for rental or sharecropping agreements (see below) rather than wage labour. The dream of owning their own land was achieved by some since about twenty per cent of African American families in the former slave states owned their own farms by the end of the nineteenth century.

The Shore family – African American homesteaders in Nebraska, 1887. Behind them are the sod houses in which they lived.

This image of an African American farmstead presents an idealised vision of life in the rural South after the Civil War. In material terms, life did not improve for most freed African Americans for many decades.

Sharecropping became more common in the South in the 1870s. Croppers of any race paid landowners a share of their crop in return for the right to work the land. They used the rest to feed themselves and buy the tools, equipment, seeds and livestock they needed. In the words of one former slave, sharecropping was more attractive than wage labour since,

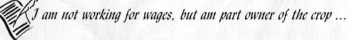

I am not working for wages, but am part owner of the crop ...

However, for most freed labourers employed in agriculture, whether or not they were sharecroppers, life remained hard.

Buffalo Soldiers

After the Civil War, African American soldiers who wanted to continue in military service were able to join one of four segregated units either in the Cavalry or Infantry. These units were stationed in the West, where they protected migrants and homesteaders, safeguarded passenger and freight transport, hunted down outlaws and participated in campaigns against Native Americans, who called them 'Buffalo soldiers'. During the Spanish-American War, African American troops served with distinction in Cuba and the Philippines.

Jim Crow

The fifty years before the First World War were made more difficult for most African Americans by racist violence and intimidation. The federal government did not act on their behalf as many were prevented from exercising their right to vote. 'Jim Crow' segregation laws were introduced to block the path to full citizenship for most African Americans in the South. These laws and rules segregated African Americans from the rest of American society in many states, and denied many their most basic civil rights. Both the National Association for the Advancement of Coloured People (NAACP) and the National Urban League (NUL) were founded in this period, to campaign for civil rights and demand that the republic provide,

freedom and justice to all.

Booker T. Washington (1856–1915), was born a slave, but became a teacher and went on to establish his own school, then college, for African Americans at Tuskegee, Alabama.

The Great Migration

By the beginning of the twentieth century, the majority of African Americans were literate and many had received degrees from institutions of higher learning. A few, like Booker T. Washington and W. E. B. DuBois had emerged as national figures in their work to achieve access to education, and full political and civil rights for other African Americans. African American artistic genius in music, painting, sculpture, literature and dance was recognised in the USA and Europe. This period also marked the beginning of the Great Migration of African Americans from the rural South to the urban, industrial North in search of new opportunities.

Marcus Garvey

The Jamaican Marcus Garvey and his Universal Negro Improvement Association (UNIA) represented a crucial phase in the African Americans' struggle for justice and equality. Garvey arrived in the USA at a time of African American discontent, marked by race riots and racial tension, and he became leader of the largest movement in African American history. The UNIA incorporated the Black Star shipping line in 1919, to transport passengers between America, the Caribbean and Africa, and to serve as a symbol of African American pride and prestige. In 1922, the federal government indicted Garvey on fraud charges – he was imprisoned, and then deported to Jamaica in 1927.

Marcus Garvey (1887–1940) drives through the streets of Harlem, New York, in a plumed hat and uniform. Garvey was a huge icon for many African Americans.

Civil Rights

The stuggle for justice was reignited in the 1950s, when Rosa Parks and other African Americans refused to give up their seats on segregated buses in Montgomery, Alabama. They sparked off a campaign against the laws that denied African Americans their full civil rights and forced them to use separate but not equal facilities. One of the civil rights campaign's leaders was a preacher called Martin Luther King, Jr. who declared that:

We have no alternative but to protest.

Martin Luther King (1929–68), seen here front row, far left, leading a vast crowd at a civil rights rally, 1963.

The African American boycott of Montgomery's buses led to their desegregation, and this was a significant step towards achieving equality for African Americans in the Deep South. Restaurants and other public places were soon desegregated, and in the 1960s, President John F. Kennedy pushed for African American students to be taught in desegregated public schools. His successor, President Lyndon B. Johnson, supported new legislation aimed at restoring full equal rights to African Americans, including the right to vote in state and federal elections.

Emancipation and Inequality in the Caribbean

Apart from freedom, emancipation brought few other benefits to freed slaves in most Spanish, Portuguese, French, Danish and Dutch colonies in South America and the Caribbean. There was no redistribution of land that would have prevented freed slaves, who had little or no education and few transferable skills, from sinking to the lower ranks of society. Economic power rested in the hands of former slave owners. Political power was shared by a small elite that consisted of those who boasted of their European ancestry, and those with a mixed race background that distanced them from the most disadvantaged freed slaves.

Saint-Domingue

The exception was the French colony of Saint-Domingue, where the leaders of a successful slave revolt had declared Saint-Domingue to be an independent republic under its alternative name of Haiti, in 1804. When Dessalines, the republic's founder died two years later, the state was divided between a former soldier called Petion, and a former slave who had bought his freedom, Henri Christophe. Between them, these men and their followers created a unique society in the Caribbean. Most slave owners and their families had fled or been killed. The ruling elite consisted of the descendants of liaisons between African slaves and their owners, the extended families of slaves who had been freed before the revolts, and those former slaves who had acted as leaders of the slave revolts between 1791 and 1804, and had been rewarded with promotion and positions of power and influence.

A Melting Pot

Following the abolition of slavery, developments in the labour market further complicated the racial composition of former colonies in South America and the Caribbean. Contract or indentured labour immigration led to large Asian populations from India and Indonesia being established in Suriname, Guyana and Trinidad, and smaller populations being settled in Jamaica and a number of other British Caribbean islands. Large-scale immigration from Spain during the first half of the twentieth century further marginalised the

These houses in Port of Spain on the Caribbean island of Trinidad remind us that for many of the descendants of the region's slave labourers, poor housing, poverty, crime and low life expectancy are facts of life.

African Caribbeans on islands such as Cuba, Puerto Rico and the Dominican Republic. Post-emancipation society in most former colonies was stratified by race and ethnic background, with former slaves and their descendants, and the surviving remnants of the region's indigenous peoples, invariably the victims of every form of discrimination and racial prejudice.

George William Gordon

A demonstration by former slaves in 1865 outside the courthouse in Morant Bay, Jamaica.

In the British colony of Jamaica, George William Gordon, the son of a plantation owner and a slave mother, had urged fellow freed slaves to protest at their lack of education and employment opportunities, in peaceful and non-violent ways. In 1865, the British put down a rising of former slaves and their families, and the Governor announced that he held Gordon responsible for the trouble, although he had not taken part in the rising. Gordon was tried for treason and hanged. It was clear that the world's leading imperial power was not prepared to listen to appeals for racial equality made by some of their Caribbean subjects. Society in British Caribbean colonies was to remain hierarchical and authoritarian for decades, based on ethnic and racial origins inherited from slave times.

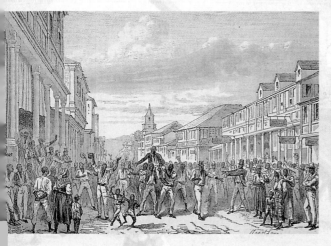

MODERN SLAVERY

Angola

Since the abolition of chattel slavery in the Americas, the term 'slavery' has been used to refer to a wide variety of human rights violations and slavery-like practices throughout the world. In many places, including Africa, forced labour or debt bondage became the modern forms of slavery that continue to blight millions of lives today.

At the beginning of the twentieth century, in the huge Portuguese colony of Angola in West Africa, a system of voluntary contracts for paid labour allowed Portuguese traders, known as labour agents, to bargain with local chiefs. In exchange for guns, ammunition, rum and other goods, the chiefs would ensure that men, women and children were handed over to plantation owners to be employed as forced labour. Henry W. Nevinson published details of this trade in 1906, and pointed out that for colonists,

the only motive for slavery is money-making, and the only argument in favour of it is that it pays.

In 1961, there was a rebellion against the system of forced labour, followed by a Portuguese campaign of terror that led to the deaths of at least 20,000 Africans. Guerrilla warfare against Portuguese rule lasted for more than twenty years until Portugal granted the colony its independence in 1975. However, various forms of forced labour or bondage exist in Africa and throughout the rest of the world today, despite legal efforts at national and international levels to abolish these practices.

Angolan rebels undergoing attack training for guerilla warfare, 1961.

Totalitarian States

Over the past 100 years, totalitarian regimes have not hesitated to use slave labour. In the USSR, Stalin used millions of political

The Nazis forced tens of thousands of their victims to work as forced or slave labour, such as these inmates of Dachau, one of the earliest concentration camps, established in 1933.

prisoners as slave labour on huge construction projects, making the captives in labour camps a key factor in his economic plans. The use of forced or 'corrective' labour declined after the dictator's death, but it continued to exist in various forms until the collapse of the Soviet Union in 1991. During the Second World War, the Nazi regime employed hundreds of thousands of Soviet prisoners of war, the inmates of labour camps, and conscripted labour from occupied Western Europe as slave labour in factories, mines and farms. According to the historian, Milton Meltzer, by 1944, there were more than seven million slaves working for the Nazis, who were,

 degraded, beaten and starved, and often left to die for lack of food, clothing and shelter.

In China, Mao's 'reform through labour' programme forced victims of the communist regime into labour reform camps in order to work on major construction projects and produce cheap consumer goods for export.

Modern Slavery

The United Nations defines slavery as the condition of someone over whom any or all of the powers attached to the right of ownership are exercised. Member states are bound to eradicate chattel slavery, serfdom, debt bondage, the exploitation of children, servile forms of marriage, forced labour and every form of sexual slavery. African nations whose populations were depleted by the slave trade have considered asking for compensation for centuries of exploitation and forced labour inflicted by European states and their former colonies.

Poverty-stricken children wait for food in a refugee camp. Throughout the world, hundreds of thousands of people have become refugees to escape the horrors of civil war.

Poverty

Evidence from the International Labour Organisation, human and civil rights groups and other investigations confirms that slavery and slavery-like practices can still be found in the world today. A common factor linking most forms of forced labour or servitude is the extreme poverty endured by so many people, whether they are agricultural labourers displaced by debt, war or climate change, or refugees fleeing political or ethnic conflict or natural disaster. Parents are often involved in slave traffic, abandoning or selling their children to traders. They hope that their sons and daughters will be employed as domestic servants or learn a useful trade, but are aware that they could become young victims of the sex industry.

Child Slavery

Despite laws passed against child slavery in many states, it has been reported that millions of children are employed as slave or forced labour in factories and workshops in the Indian subcontinent. Children as young as six or seven can be forced to work for fourteen hours per day in textile factories. They are frequently beaten, and are too terrified of what might happen to them if they run away from the employer who paid their parents for their bonded labour. In South America, forest clearance and other environmentally-destructive enterprises often use debt bondage to obtain labour. Impoverished rural workers are allowed to run up debts to pay for their transport to the remote forests where they have been promised work. Their wages are held back to pay for debts owed to the company for equipment, accommodation and food.

Throughout the world, modern lightweight weapons have enabled children to be used in combat as child soldiers. Many more children have been used by armed forces as spies, messengers, servants and prostitutes. Some children have been kidnapped and recruited forcibly into armies and guerrilla groups, but others have been driven into the military by poverty and abuse at the hands of employers and occupying forces. Some governments and armed groups use children because they believe that they are easier to condition, with or without the use of alcohol and drugs, into unthinking obedience. Most child soldiers are aged between fourteen and eighteen, but many are recruited from the age of ten or even younger. Girls and boys are at risk of rape, sexual harassment and abuse.

Boys training as guerrillas at a secret base in Eritrea represent the modern face of slavery for many children. These boys would have had little or no say in their adoption by the soldiers who control their lives, and who could order them to their deaths in battle.

Global Economics

Pressure groups have expressed concern at what they regard as the abuse of power by the world's leading nations, and the growing poverty in many nations, as governments, multinational companies and world bodies appeared to globalise capital and economic development. Campaigners have tried to encourage consumers to boycott goods produced by forced or bonded labour, and turn concern into action against exploitative labour practices and their consequences for the health and welfare of their victims.

Distance and primitive communications allowed eighteenth-century consumers to ignore the horrors of slavery and the slave trade. Consumers in the twenty-first century, however, have knowledge about the horrors of modern slavery at their fingertips, due to the revolution in communications technology that has taken place since the 1970s.

David Livingstone (1813–73) worked as a child in a Scottish textile mill, and went on to become a Christian missionary who campaigned against the horrors of the African slave trade in the second half of the nineteenth century.

Who Bears the Blame?

In the nineteenth century, Christian missionaries and explorers, such as David Livingstone, wrote accounts of their expeditions into the African interior and raised public awareness in Europe and North America of the atrocities committed by slave traders. These missionaries, confident of their moral superiority over Africans, worked to abolish slavery and the slave trade, and reshape African society to the European model, by supporting the colonisation of Africa.

At the beginning of the twenty-first century, a number of South American, Caribbean and African states called for the United Nations to declare colonialism and slavery to be crimes against humanity. They also demanded reparations, or compensation, for the long-term effects that slavery and colonialism have had on so many regions. They accused the United States and many European countries of being largely responsible for the poverty and racial tensions that have blighted so many lives.

In response, some former colonial powers claimed that the horrors of slavery and the slave trade were not region-specific. They used as evidence the long-established slave trade between Africa and Asia. States opposed to the demand for reparations suggested that they would be prepared to acknowledge a moral obligation to those countries that suffered from slavery and colonisation. Several former colonial powers said that some, but not all, aspects of colonialism had been damaging. This suggests that there is still some way to go before paternalistic attitudes towards Africa and South America are extinguished in some parts of Europe and North America.

GLOSSARY

abolitionists supporters of various campaigns to end the slave trade, or slavery, when the legal slave trade had been abolished

bills of exchange bills that traders received for slaves, which could be exchanged for cargoes of plantation produce that would fetch high prices in Europe

Black Codes laws originally introduced to prevent slave rebellions, but by the time of American independence had developed to control every aspect of slave life

colony an area of land that another country controls, and often settles in, with or without the full co-operation of the area's original population

Confederacy the Confederate States of America, set up by the states that seceded from the United States in the 1860s, but defeated in 1865

contrabands slaves living in territory captured by Union forces, or runaway slaves who reached Union forces during the American Civil War; war contraband was any enemy property that was captured by military action

dysentery a disease causing severe diarrhoea that often killed African captives on the Middle Passage, due to the effects of dehydration

emancipation the setting free of slaves

Enlightenment eighteenth-century intellectual movement that believed that rational, critical study and analysis should be applied in all matters

feudal rights a medieval landlord's right to service in the form of work, goods or other duties

gang system a system of field labour on large plantations in which gangs of slaves perform various tasks according to their age, fitness and skills

guerrilla irregular, often ill-trained soldiers who use ambush and hit-and-run tactics against better-trained, more powerful opponents

indentured servants servants who signed a contract that bound them to work for a master for a set number of years in return for food and shelter, and possibly training or transportation to a colony

Indian territory the vast area of North America, west of the Mississippi River, that would be settled by millions of migrants in the fifty years after the American Civil War; most of the tribes that inhabited this land would be attacked, defeated and consigned to their own limited territory or reservations by the last decade of the nineteenth century

Jim Crow a term to describe the vast number of laws, rules and regulations that segregated African Americans from other Americans in the years following the American Civil War, up to the 1960s

maroons freed slaves and runaways in remote regions of the Americas who maintained their independence from the slave-owning communities close to where they lived

Middle Passage the journey undertaken by African captives to the Americas by ship

plantation a large area of land on which a single crop, such as sugar, tobacco or cotton, is grown

reconstruction the programme of aid directed at the defeated Confederacy at the end of the American Civil War, in the hope that the former slave states could be restored quickly to full membership of the Union

republic government without a monarchy, but by an appointed or elected head of state

sectionalism the division of communities or political life along rigid lines based on a single issue that forces groups to ignore what they have in common with each other

serfdom a medieval form of forced labour, where farm labourers and their families worked for a landowner, had few legal rights, and were not allowed to leave their place of work without the permission of the landowner

sharecropping a form of agriculture in which tenant farmers promised a share of their next crop to their landowner in return for credit to purchase seeds, tools and other resources

slave-driver an assistant to a slave owner or overseer, who supervised the work of a slave gang; often, the driver was a trusted slave who received privileges for performing this role

slave overseer an assistant to the slave owner who supervised the work of the slave-drivers and the slaves

smallpox an infectious disease that was common in Europe until the nineteenth century, and caused the deaths of millions throughout the world until it was eradicated in the second half of the twentieth century

staple one of the main or usual crops grown in a particular area

trading factories fortified settlements where European merchants traded with local merchants and traders, guarded by European and local troops

transportation a form of punishment by which convicted criminals are used as forced labour in a colony or settlement for a set number of years

Underground Railroad an informal network of more than 3,000 sympathetic people who broke the law by assisting slaves escape to freedom in the Northern states, or Canada

TIMELINE OF EVENTS

1492	Christopher Columbus made landfall in what would become known as the Caribbean or West Indies
1500	Portugal took possession of Brazil
1655	Jamaican slaves formed first large maroon community
1761	Society of Friends banned people engaged in the slave trade from membership
1772	British ruling against forcing a runaway slave to leave UK
1787	Free African Society formed, USA; Society for the Abolition of the Slave Trade founded, UK
1791	Extension of French Declaration of the Rights of Man to include freed slaves and their descendants, but not slaves; slave revolt in Saint-Domingue
1794	Slavery abolished in all French colonies
1802	Napoleon I restored slavery in all French colonies
1804	Saint-Domingue declared its independence
1807	British ended slave trade in British ships
1815	Most leading European states affirmed their opposition to the slave trade
1820	Missouri Compromise, USA
1831	Nat Turner's slave revolt, USA
1833	American Anti-Slavery Society founded
1834	Slavery abolished throughout British Empire

1848	All slaves freed in the French and Danish colonies
1854	Kansas–Nebraska Act, USA
1857	Dred Scott Case, USA
1859	John Brown's attempt at slave revolt in Virginia, USA
1861	American Civil War began
1863	Emancipation Proclamation, USA
1865	American Civil War ended; Thirteenth Amendment to the US Constitution; British put down a rising of former slaves in Jamaica
1866	Civil Rights Act, USA
1885	King Leopold II of Belgium took personal control of the Congo Free State; Europe's major powers agreed guidelines for the further colonisation of Africa
1886	Slavery in Spain's colonies ended
1888	Slavery abolished in Brazil
1890	Seventeen major powers agreed to put an end to African slavery
1944	Seven million Nazi slaves employed in Europe
1945	United Nations established
1950s	Labour reform camps in China; American civil rights campaigns
1961	Rebellion against forced labour in Angola
1964	Martin Luther King, Jr. awarded Nobel Peace Prize
1975	Angolan independence
1991	USSR collapsed, ending forced labour

FURTHER INFORMATION

Of the thousands of books about the transatlantic slave trade, slavery in the Americas and its abolition, and the aftermath of abolition in the nineteenth and twentieth centuries for the Americas and Africa, the following are among the best starting points:

S. Drescher and S. L. Engerman, *A Historical Guide to World Slavery*, Oxford University Press, Oxford, 1998
David Eltis, *Economic Growth and the Ending of the Transatlantic Slave Trade*, Oxford University Press, Oxford, 1987
Peter Kolchin, *American Slavery*, Penguin, London, 1995
James M. McPherson, *Battle Cry of Freedom: the Civil War Era*, Oxford University Press, Oxford, 1988
Milton Meltzer, *Slavery, A World History*, Da Capo Press, New York, 1993

There are many interesting and useful websites that contain reliable information on the slave trade and related topics.
www.spartacus.schoolnet.co.uk/USAslavery.htm
amistad.mysticseaport.org
www.middlepassage.org
www.loc.gov
www.history.rochester.edu
www.princeton.edu
www.antislavery.org

INDEX

THE GREATEST
INVENTIONS
OF ALL TIME

Jillian Powell

WAYLAND

First published in Great Britain in 2015 by Wayland
Copyright © Wayland, 2015
All rights reserved.

Dewey Number: 600-dc23

Printed in China

ISBN: 978 0 7502 9212 2
Ebook ISBN: 978 0 7502 9545 1
10 9 8 7 6 5 4 3 2 1

Wayland
An imprint of Hachette Children's Group
Part of Hodder & Stoughton
Carmelite House
50 Victoria Embankment
London EC4Y 0DZ

An Hachette UK Company
www.hachette.co.uk
www.hachettechildrens.co.uk

Editor: Elizabeth Brent
Designer: Elaine Wilkinson
Researchers: Hester Vaizey and Edward Field
at The National Archives

The National Archives, London, England.
www.nationalarchives.gov.uk

The National Archives looks after the UK government's historical documents. It holds records dating back nearly 1,000 years from the time of William the Conqueror's Domesday Book to the present day. All sorts of documents are stored there, including letters, photographs, maps and posters. They include great Kings and Queens, famous rebels like Guy Fawkes and the strange and unusual – such as reports of UFOs and even a mummified rat!

Material reproduced courtesy of The National Archives: Front cover: (bottom left) BT 45/2 (205) Syringe 1844-1845, (centre) COPY 1/95 (294) Ladies riding Penny Farthing bycycles 1891, (top right) AIR1/2450 Glider invented by Sir Hiram Maxim and Lt Dunne 1915 (1); p3: (bottom left) MFC 1/203 (47) Robert Stephenson's specification for an improvement in locomotive engines, December 1833; p4: COPY 1/545 Short-Wright biplane 1910; p8: (bottom left) C 73/15 m50 Richard Arkwright's 1776 specification for devices to prepare silk and cotton for a spinning machine; p9: (top) C 73/13 m31 Richard Arkwright's 1769 specification for a spinning machine, the water frame; p11 (top) COAL 13/115 George Stephenson, buried in Holy Trinity Church, Chesterfield, 1907-1913, (bottom) MFC 1/203 (47) Robert Stephenson's specification for an improvement in locomotive engines, December 1833; p12: (top) COPY 1/95 (294) Ladies riding Penny Farthing bycycles 1891, (bottom) COPY 1/440 (i) (18) Sparks and Martins bicycle carrying three men with two more bicycles, 1899; p13: (bottom) MUN 5/394 (57) Big Willie also called Centipede or Mother Tank January 1916; p14: (top) MT 95/52 Reflecting road studs plans (cover) August 1952, (bottom) MT 95/52 (11) Catseyes road studs test with tank tracks 1945; p15: (top) MT 95/154 (3) Pedestrian crossing test markings c1949, (middle) AIR 62/1017 Whittle jet engine (6) 1942-1943, (bottom) AIR 62/1017 Whittle jet engine (7) 1942-1943; p17: (top) COPY 1/471 Thomas Edison 1904; p18: (top) BT 42/12 (1197) Parachute machine for sweeping chimnies 1850, (bottom) COPY 1/369/243 Chimney sweep, 1884; p21: (top) BT 45/2 (205) Syringe 1844-1845, (bottom) BT 45/2 (354) Life Buoy 1845; p28: CAB 163/230 (1) Colossus computer; p30: (bottom) COPY 1/95 (294) Ladies riding Penny Farthing bycycles 1891

Picture credits: Front cover: (top left) BlazJ/Shutterstock.com, (bottom centre) Dja65/Shutterstock.com, (bottom right) Grafissimo/iStock.com, (right centre) Back cover: (top left) Wikicommons, (bottom left) Wikicommons/The Wellcome Trust, (bottom right) Igor Golovniov/Shutterstock.com, p3: (right) Bryan Donkin Archive Trust/Science Museum/Science & Society Picture Library; p5: (top) Anna Abramskaya/Shutterstock.com; p6: (top) Getty Images/Hulton Archive; p7: (top) Oticki/Shutterstock.com, (bottom) Bocman/Shutterstock.com; p8: (top) Joseph Wright/Wikimedia Commons; p9: (bottom) Clem Rutter/Wikimedia Commons; p10: (top) duncan1890/iStock, (bottom) Igor Golovniov/Shutterstock.com; p13: (top) Boyer/Getty Images; p16: (top) Getty Images/Science and Society Picture Library, (bottom) Getty Images/Science and Society Picture Library; p17: (bottom) Gateshead Council/Wikimedia Commons; p19: (top) Chippix/Shutterstock.com, (bottom) Wellcome Images/Wikimedia Commons; p20: (top) Georgios Kollidas/Shutterstock.com, (bottom) Getty Images/Science and Society Picture Library; (top) Bryan Donkin Archive Trust/Science Museum/Science & Society Picture Library; p23: (top) Getty Images/UniversalImagesGroup, (bottom) Georgios Kollidas/Shutterstock.com; p24: (left) Wikimedia Commons, (right) Doctor Jools/Shutterstock.com; p25: (top) Wikimedia Commons, (bottom right) US Department of the Interior. Patent Office; p26: (top) National Media Museum/Science & Society Picture Library, (bottom) Ivan_Sabo/Shutterstock.com, Photo smile/Shutterstock.com; p27: (top) Daily Herald Archive/National Media Museum/Science & Society Picture Library, (bottom) Amnarj Tanongrattana/Shutterstock.com; p29: (top) drserg/Shutterstock.com, (bottom) Yentafern/Shutterstock.com; p31 (top) Igor Golovniov/Shutterstock.com. All other graphics and background elements courtesy of Shutterstock.com

Please note:
The website addresses (URLs) included in this book were valid at the time of going to press. However, because of the nature of the Internet, it is possible that some addresses may have changed, or sites may have changed or closed down since publication. While the author and publishers regret any inconvenience this may cause to the readers, no responsibility for any such changes can be accepted by either the author or the publishers.

Contents

Incredible inventions

The greatest inventions change people's lives forever. Imagine life without the option to ride your bicycle, or travel by car, train or plane. Think what the world would be like without radio, television or the Internet. Many of the most revolutionary inventions have become part of our everyday lives, and we now take them for granted. For example, it is only when there is a power cut that we can imagine how shadowy and dark life was, before the invention of electric lighting.

The most incredible inventions can come from humble beginnings, or great catastrophes. The printing press, which changed the world in 1439 because it meant books could be printed over and over again, rather than laboriously handwritten, was modelled on wooden olive and wine presses used in the Mediterranean. The aeroplane was developed during World War I, for use in spy and bombing missions, but went on to make overseas travel fast and affordable. Wars often lead to new discoveries and inventions.

Some inventions go back further than you might think, too. Did you know that the Romans invented concrete and under-floor heating, or that wigs were invented in Ancient Egypt?

This book looks at the amazing people and incredible stories behind some of the greatest inventions of all time, and at how they went on to change the world.

Inventors can risk their lives carrying out dangerous experiments to develop their idea. Some have even been killed by their own inventions, such as Horace Lawson Hunley, who invented the first combat submarine but died when it sank on a test mission.

Down on the farm

In 1701, an inventor named Jethro Tull created an incredible machine called a seed drill. It became part of a revolution in farming methods and practices known as the Agricultural Revolution. Tull's seed drill used horsepower to mechanize the process of planting seeds, making it more efficient and meaning farmers could produce more food in greater quantities than before!

The seed drill

Jethro Tull was born into a wealthy farming family in Berkshire in 1674. He travelled to Europe to learn about new farming methods. When he returned, he designed a mechanical seed drill, and built the first model using foot pedals from his local church organ. At that time, people sowed seed by hand, and it was often wasted, or fell unevenly, making it difficult to weed between plants as they grew.

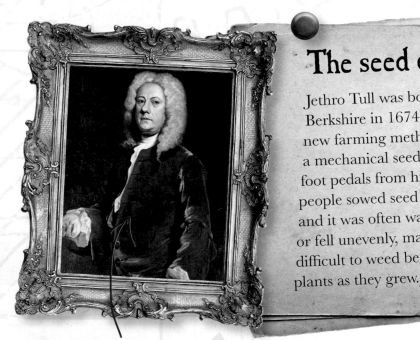

A portrait of Tull, painted around 1720

An engraving of Tull's design for the seed drill

The seed drill sowed faster and more efficiently, and meant that the plants grew in straight rows. The machine had a plough at the front to cut straight furrows into the soil at the right depth. The seeds passed through a funnel into the furrow, then a harrow at the back covered them with soil. Three seed drills operating side by side could increase crop production by up to eight times.

A farmer using a more modern seed drill

Mechanizing farming

The seed drill did not change farming overnight. Tull mistakenly believed that soil could provide plants with all the nutrients they needed, and dismissed the idea of fertilizers. The drill was expensive, and could be unreliable. However, by introducing mechanization, it began a revolution in farming methods which ultimately led to the development of the farm machinery we use today, such as tractors, combine harvesters and rotovators. Modern farmers still use seed drills, too, but they look quite different from Tull's original design – and they no longer rely on the foot pedals from dismantled church organs!

An early version of the seed drill

In the 1960s, a group of British musicians decided to name their band after Jethro Tull! The band was successful for more than 40 years, touring and releasing albums, before splitting up in 2014.

Industrial power

The Industrial Revolution swept through Britain in the 18th and 19th centuries, transforming the country from a rural economy into a manufacturing superpower. It was largely the result of the development of new machinery, including the spinning frame. Created by an inventor named Richard Arkwright in 1768, this revolutionized the production of cotton cloth.

A portrait of Richard Arkwright, painted in 1790

Spinning frame

For centuries, cotton had been hand spun, but the threads were weak and irregular and had to be woven with expensive linen to make strong cloth. Arkwright recruited a clockmaker named John Kay and a team of craftsmen to build a prototype for a spinning frame. It had three pairs of rollers turning at different speeds. As they produced yarn, spindles twisted the fibres together, making a strong, regular thread. Arkwright tried horses, then water wheels, to power the frame. In 1771, he opened a factory next to the River Derwent in Cromford, Derbyshire.

Arkwright's design for a machine to prepare thread for spinning

WANTED AT CROMFORD

FRAMEWORK-KNITTERS AND WEAVERS WITH LARGE FAMILIES. Likewise children of all ages may have constant employment.

ADVERT IN THE *DERBY MERCURY*, SEPTEMBER 1781.

A plan for Arkwright's spinning frame, from 1769

Father of factories

Women and children worked in the spinning factory while weavers worked at home, turning the yarn into cloth. Two-thirds of Arkwright's workers were children, some as young as six. More factories followed in Lancashire, Staffordshire and Scotland, powered by water and later steam, and Arkwright became known as the 'Father of Factories'. Many people criticized Arkwright's invention because it put skilled hand spinners out of work and relied on long hours of child labour. But the fast, cheap production of cotton cloth heralded a new factory age. By 1871, one-third of all the world's cotton cloth was produced in Manchester and the towns and villages surrounding it, and the city was nicknamed 'Cottonopolis'.

Arkwright was born in Preston, Lancashire, in 1732. His family could not afford to send him to school so he was taught to read and write by a cousin. He became a barber's apprentice and in 1762 set up his own wig-making business, travelling around the country to collect real hair for his wigs. It was on his travels that he met John Kay.

A spinning frame, now in a museum in Manchester, England

9

Full steam ahead

In the 19th century, the world was changed forever by the invention of steam power. Prior to this, the only transport available was either animal-powered, for example horses and carts, or weather-dependent, such as sailboats. Steam power made it possible for people to travel faster, further, more safely and comfortably, and also made it quicker, easier and cheaper to transport goods around the country.

The steam engine

Richard Trevithick, born in Cornwall in 1771, was known as 'the Cornish Giant' because he was over 6 feet (1.83m) tall. He became an engineer in the mine where his father worked. Here he began working on the idea of a compact engine, powered by steam under high pressure, that could run on roads or railways. In 1801, he demonstrated a full-sized locomotive, the *Puffing Devil*, taking six friends for a test ride. Although things didn't always go entirely to plan, as the letter below demonstrates, Trevithick's invention of 'strong' or high-power steam meant that compact, portable steam engines could be used in mines, on farms, in factories, on ships and on locomotives.

Trevithick made high-pressure steam 'portable'

Trevithick's design for a high-power steam engine

"Yesterday we proceeded on our journey with the engine. We performed the 9 miles in 4 hours and 5 minutes. We had to remove some large rocks on the way. On our return home one of the small bolts that fastened the axle to the boiler broke, and all the water ran out of the boiler."

Letter to Davies Gilbert, February 1804

The passenger railway

George Stephenson was born into a poor family in Wylam, near Newcastle-upon-Tyne, in 1781. Employed as a mechanic in a coalmine, he worked with his son Robert and a friend, Henry Booth, to design and build a steam-powered locomotive that could run on iron rails. *The Rocket* was entered into trials held by the Liverpool and Manchester Railway Company to find the best engine to run between the two cities. On the day of the trials, 15,000 people came to watch the locomotives race. *The Rocket* reached speeds of 24 miles per hour (39 km/h), and was declared the winner.

George Stephenson, painted towards the end of his life

Stephenson's locomotive designs

11

Reinventing the wheel

The wheel has been around for thousands of years — the earliest depiction of a wheeled wagon is on a pot dating from around 3500–3350 BCE, that was excavated in modern-day Poland. However, three inventors took the wheel and used it as a basis for their own, revolutionary, inventions.

Women racing on penny-farthings in 1891

The safety bicycle

John Starley was a gardener's son, born in Essex in 1854. When he was 18, he moved to Coventry to work with his uncle James, who designed bicycles and tricycles. James Starley's designs were an improvement on the earlier 'high wheelers', known as penny-farthings, which had no gears or pedals and gave a bumpy, uncomfortable ride, dangerous at high speeds. In 1885, John designed the first 'safety bicycle', called the 'Rover', which was lighter and cheaper to buy. It made cycling an affordable way to travel for pleasure and sport.

The safety bicycle had nearly equal-sized wheels

Pneumatic tyres

In 1887, John Boyd Dunlop, a vet working in Belfast, invented an air-filled tyre for his son's tricycle by cutting up an old garden hose and pumping it full of air. Prior to this, tyres were made either from wood or iron, or from solid rubber. Dunlop patented the idea for inflatable rubber tyres, which improved wheel grip on roads, and gave a smoother, safer ride at high speeds. In 1889, he set up the Dunlop business and when a local cyclist, Willie Hume, won a race using the new tyres, they quickly became popular for bicycles and later cars.

Dunlop's son trying out air-filled tyres on his tricycle

The military tank

Sir Ernest Swinton was born in India in 1868, and acted as the government's official war correspondent in World War I. Witnessing trench warfare first hand, he saw soldiers being killed in their thousands by machine gun fire as they advanced towards enemy lines. When he saw tractors pulling guns to the front line, he had the idea of building armoured vehicles running on caterpillar tracks. A "Landships" Committee was appointed to design and build the vehicles in top secret, and the first tank went into battle in 1916. They became important weapons, because they could move over difficult and muddy ground and advance into enemy territory whilst keeping soldiers safe from enemy fire.

Tanks are named after water tanks – when the British Army first began using them on the battlefield, they pretended they were carrying water to the troops, so the enemy wouldn't guess what their brand-new weapons were.

Transforming transport

In the 20th century, three inventions altered transport forever. Two – cat's eyes and the zebra crossing – made Britain's roads dramatically safer. The third – Frank Whittle's jet engine – made travel by air faster and easier than ever before.

REFLECTING
ROAD STUDS
LTD.
BOOTHTOWN, HALIFAX.
ENGLAND

A 1950s book of plans for road studs

Cat's eyes

Percy Shaw left school in Yorkshire in 1903 at the age of 13. He began work repairing roads, using a mechanical roller he built himself from an old engine and lorry wheels. He was driving home one night in 1933, when he saw his headlights reflected in the eyes of a cat by the roadside. He began working on road studs to help guide motorists on dark roads.

Shaw experimented until he reached the design he patented in 1934, opening his own factory in 1935. During blackouts to deter bombing raids in World War II, the British government realised the value of road studs, and soon millions of cat's eyes were being used in Britain and all around the world.

Shaw became famous as an eccentric millionaire inventor, living in a house without curtains, carpets or much furniture, but keeping three televisions running constantly, all with the sound turned down.

Tanks were used to test how robust the studs were

The zebra crossing

Two million cars were using Britain's roads by the 1950s, and road traffic was increasing rapidly. Metal studs and flashing beacons were the only markings for pedestrian crossings and, with road accidents on the rise, the Ministry of Transport carried out trials to find the most effective crossings. The most successful design, the black-and-white striped zebra crossing, was introduced in 1951.

A prototype jet engine

The jet engine

In 1931, Frank Whittle was a 24-year-old fighter pilot with the Royal Air Force when he invented a new kind of aircraft engine. His turbo jet engine replaced pistons and propellers with a rotating gas turbine and air compressor. Whittle struggled to fund his new idea but, in 1937, private sponsors helped him develop the engine, which the Air Ministry adopted after successful test flights. The engine introduced a new jet age, because it made planes much more powerful, and able to travel much more quickly.

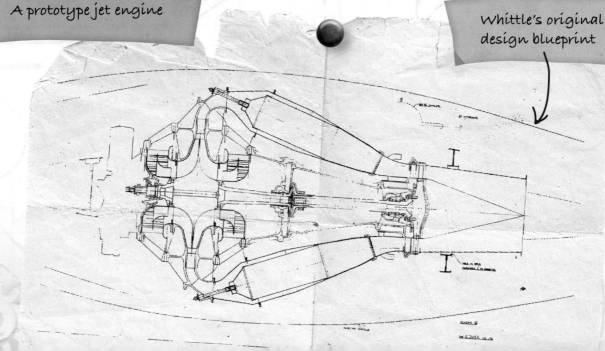

Whittle's original design blueprint

Close to home

Imagine what life would be like if you couldn't turn on an electric light at the flick of a switch, or flush a toilet! From the 18th century onwards, inventions from the light bulb to the vacuum cleaner revolutionized domestic life in Britain.

The flushing toilet

The idea for a flushing toilet developed over centuries. In the ancient civilizations of the Indus Valley and Ancient Rome, running water was used to clear away toilet waste. Queen Elizabeth I's godson, Sir John Harington, designed a water closet for her in 1596 but many people made fun of the idea – preferring to use holes in the ground, or chamber pots! It was not until 1775 that a patent was granted, to a man named Alexander Cummings, for a flushing toilet. Joseph Bramah, a locksmith and cabinetmaker from Yorkshire who installed water closets designed by Cummings, patented an improved design in 1778.

Bramah's other inventions included a beer machine and a hydraulic press

Bramah's 1778 design for a valve toilet

The light bulb

Before electricity, people relied on candles, or gas or oil lamps, for light. A chemist from Sunderland, Joseph Swan, began experiments to create an electric light. He passed electricity through a carbon rod, making it glow inside a sealed glass bulb. In 1878, Swan gave a public demonstration of his lamps in Newcastle-upon-Tyne, but the bulbs only lasted 12 hours and the light was poor. An American scientist, Thomas Edison, improved the design and in 1883, Edison Electric and the Swan Electric Light Company merged to begin manufacturing electric lighting.

Thomas Edison

Joseph Swan at work

The vacuum cleaner

Hubert Cecil Booth, an engineer born in Gloucester in 1871, was watching a train being cleaned by a machine blowing air when he had the idea of a vacuum cleaner that could suck up and contain the dust. Booth's machine replaced dustpans, brushes and carpet beaters but it was so large that the pump, powered by oil and later electricity, had to be pulled on a horse cart. Long hoses ran from the pumps into houses through the door or windows.

Booth demonstrated his idea at a restaurant with some friends, placing a handkerchief onto a chair back and sucking through it, to show how it collected dust inside!

17

Easy living

Some inventions have altered domestic life in Britain, making it easier and more comfortable for many people. From the chimney sweeps' rods that meant children no longer had to climb chimneys to sweep them, to the lawnmower, which enabled grass to be cut mechanically, these inventions are still used today.

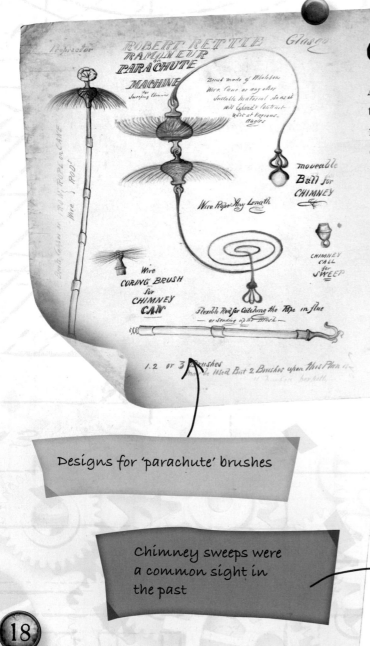

Chimney sweeps' rods

As the Industrial Revolution brought coal power to homes and factories, more and more chimneys needed cleaning. Chimney sweeps used small children, aged six or even younger, to climb up inside the chimneys to clean away soot. By the early 1800s, there were calls to replace them with machines. In 1828, Joseph Glass, an engineer from Bristol, improved an earlier idea for a system of canes and brushes, pushed up the chimney through a cloth sleeve.

Designs for 'parachute' brushes

Chimney sweeps were a common sight in the past

A woman using an early lawnmower

The lawnmower

Edwin Budding was born in Stroud in 1796, and worked as a machinist in a cotton mill. It was a machine there that, in 1830, gave him the idea for a lawnmower. For centuries, grass had been grazed by sheep or cut using hand scythes. Budding's machine made it faster and easier to cut lawns and sports fields. Used together with heavy, cast-iron lawn rollers, it encouraged the Victorian fashion for neat, striped lawns as well as sports such as lawn tennis and croquet.

The toothbrush

William Addis was a London trader who collected rags to sell for papermaking. In 1770, he was imprisoned after being caught up in a street riot, and whilst in prison, he had the idea of making brushes for cleaning teeth. Until then, people used split twigs or rags, and coal dust, soot or salt instead of toothpaste. Addis made his first brush by drilling holes into a meat bone and pushing animal bristles into it. After he was released, he set up a company in 1780, and made his fortune manufacturing toothbrushes. The first mass-produced toothbrushes were made with bone handles and boar bristles or badger hair.

An 18th-century toothbrush

Safe and sound

Clever inventions can be small objects with enormous power. From Humphry Davy's safety lamp, which saved the lives of countless miners, to the hypodermic syringe, which is still used constantly in modern medicine, these inventions were not just life changing, but life saving.

The safety lamp

In 1815, a group of Newcastle miners sent a letter to Sir Humphry Davy, a Cornish chemist and inventor, about the dangers they faced from flammable gases in the coalmines. The candles they wore on their hard hats could spark deadly explosions if they ignited gases such as methane underground. Davy experimented with several models before producing a lamp with a wire mesh around a wick that burned oil. Enough oxygen could reach the flame to keep it alight, but the mesh stopped it from igniting flammable gases.

Davy was knighted in 1812 in recognition of his services to science

Design sketches for the safety lamp

The hypodermic syringe

In 1853, Alexander Wood, a doctor from Edinburgh, used the idea of a bee sting to invent a 'hypodermic' syringe, which had a hollow needle for injecting drugs into the bloodstream. The syringes were at first used for injecting morphine as a painkiller; but their use in medicine was limited due to the lack of injectable drugs available at that time. Today, however, hypodermic syringes are used for everything from blood transfusions to vaccinations and taking blood for blood tests.

Early syringes were made of metal or glass

The inflatable life jacket

In the 19th century, inventors patented designs for inflatable life preservers, including rings, body vests, armlets and shoes. An American merchant, Peter Markus, invented an inflatable life jacket made from rubberized cloth, with air pockets that could be inflated by pulling a cord to release liquid carbon dioxide from two small cartridges. A fellow American, Andrew Toti, then improved the design using straps to keep the jackets in place. When he died in 2005, he was credited with their invention, until Markus' son wrote to *The New York Times*, giving proof of his father's patents.

A design for a life buoy from 1845

Food and drink

Inventors and inventions have transformed how, and what, we eat. From contraptions that allow food to be stored for long periods, to devices that keep it hot or cold, our diet today would be very different without them. Some inventions have even resulted in completely new foods, or in the ability to mechanically replicate existing foodstuffs, such as carbonated water.

The tin can

Before the invention of tin cans, food could only be preserved by bottling it in brine, salting and drying it, or potting it with animal fat. In 1810, a British merchant named Peter Durand patented the idea of using tin-coated cans that could be sealed and boiled to sterilize the contents. Canned foods quickly became popular with the Army and Navy and explorers on long expeditions. Durand sold his patent to Bryan Donkin, who began manufacturing canned foods for people to store at home.

The first cans were heavy, and tricky to open

The can opener was not invented for another 40 years after the tin can, and the first cans were so thick they had to be opened with a hammer and chisel!

The vacuum flask

Sir James Dewar, a Scottish chemist and physicist, was working on experiments to cool and liquefy gases when, in 1892, he invented a vacuum flask that could keep liquefied gases at low temperatures. He used two flasks, one inside the other, made from glass painted with reflective metal, with a sealed vacuum between them. This insulated the contents from the outside air temperature, keeping them hot or cold. Dewar failed to patent the idea, and in 1904, the German firm Thermos began manufacturing the flasks for home use, to keep drinks or food hot or cold.

Sir James Dewar, holding one of his vacuum flasks

Carbonated water

People had been drinking naturally occurring carbonated water, where carbon dioxide dissolves in mineral water and makes it fizzy, for thousands of years. However, in 1767, English chemist Joseph Priestley successfully dissolved carbon dioxide in water to make artificially carbonated water. This paved the way for the manufacture of fizzy drinks such as Coca Cola and lemonade.

Joseph Priestley is also credited with the discovery of oxygen

Changing communication

The way we communicate with each other today is constantly evolving with the development of new technology and media, but it was in the 19th century that inventors paved the way for modern methods of communication.

The postage stamp

Writing letters was once the only way that people could stay in touch with each other from a distance. People had to pay for letters when they received them, according to the distance they had travelled and the number of sheets they contained. Some people even tried to cut costs by writing both ways across the paper! In 1839, Rowland Hill, a retired teacher, invented the idea of adhesive postage stamps, to be paid for by the sender, and priced by the weight of the letter. The first stamps were the Penny Black and the Twopence Blue.

Rowland Hill is credited with founding the modern postal service

A Penny Black stamp

Telephone

Sometimes, inventors race against each other to file a patent for the same invention. The Scot Alexander Graham Bell patented his telephone device in 1876, hours before an American, Elisha Gray, applied for a patent. Bell was living in Boston when he made the discovery that sounds could be sent along a wire. Working with Thomas Watson, who was an expert in the new technology of electricity, he found that a wire that connected two springs could carry the sound of vibrations from one spring to the other, in the form of electrical waves. Bell and Watson went on to develop a working model of a telephone and in 1877 set up the Bell Telephone Company.

Alexander Graham Bell

An early wall-telephone

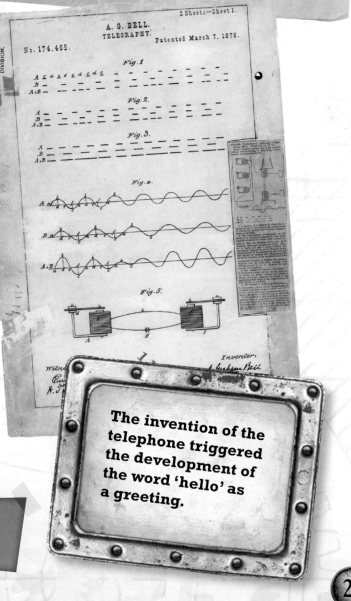

The invention of the telephone triggered the development of the word 'hello' as a greeting.

Instant images

Nowadays, watching television, or taking a picture on a smartphone, is so commonplace that we think nothing of it. So imagine having to rely on an artist's impression to show you what something looks or looked like! Before photography and televisions were invented, drawing, painting or engraving images were the only ways to capture, keep and transmit them.

Fox Talbot at home in Lacock Abbey, in Wiltshire

Photography

William Henry Fox Talbot was an English politician, scientist and inventor. He was on his honeymoon in Italy in 1833 when he had the idea of a light-sensitive machine that could automatically record the scenery he was trying to sketch. In France, the amateur scientists Joseph Niépce and Louis Daguerre had been experimenting with ways of fixing images using light on silver plate, but fixing one image took several hours and the original could not be reproduced.

When he returned home, Fox Talbot began experiments into a way of printing a photographic image on light-sensitive paper using chemicals to produce a 'negative'. This process meant an image could be printed over and over again from the same negative, and was the basis for photography for the next 150 years. It was not overtaken until the development of digital photography in the 1980s.

Examples of cameras through the ages

The television

John Logie Baird was a Scottish engineer, born in 1888. He began inventing when he was still at school, setting up an electric telephone exchange connecting his house with four friends' houses. It had to be dismantled when a low-hanging wire caused a taxi driver to have an accident.

While he was still living in his parents' house, Baird began working on the idea of capturing and transmitting live images, burning his hands during one experiment. In 1923, he managed to create a working television using spare materials including an old tea chest, a hat box and some bicycle light lenses.

Baird became the first person to demonstrate a working model of a television, transmitting black and white images, in 1926. But by 1936, a rival company, Marconi-EMI, introduced a superior electronic system. The following year, the BBC adopted the Marconi system, which was used for nearly 50 years. Although disappointed, Baird went on to experiment with colour and even 3D television.

Early televisions were large and bulky

27

Clever calculators

Can you imagine a world without computers or the Internet, where the only way of communicating with people was by letter, telephone call, or face-to-face? It seems impossible now, but it was only in the late 20th century that these inventions made the instant global exchange of information and ideas a reality.

A Colossus computer

The Colossus computer

Tommy Flowers was an engineer working with the General Post Office when his research unit was moved to Bletchley Park during World War II. They were given the task of detecting and deciphering secret codes used by the Germans for their war plans. In 1943, he began work on a machine to decipher the German Lorenz code, funding it with his own money. The Colossus machine could read 5,000 characters a minute, and was the world's first electronic, digital and programmable computer. Ten Colossus machines were built, deciphering top-secret information that helped to win the war, but although Flowers had introduced the computer age, the technology remained a military secret for decades.

The World Wide Web

British computer scientist Tim Berners-Lee was working at CERN, the European Physics Laboratory, when he had the idea of using the Internet, a global network of computers, to create the World Wide Web. This involved linking web pages using 'hypertext' – text containing links to other text. This way of linking documents had been used on single computers since the 1960s, but in 1989 Berners-Lee had the idea to link documents on computers around the world, allowing the free and global exchange of information. He created the first live web page in 1991, giving instructions on how to search and post web pages. A new age of invention had arrived.

Tim Berners-Lee speaking at a 2012 conference in the USA

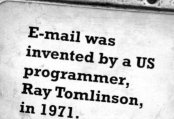

E-mail was invented by a US programmer, Ray Tomlinson, in 1971.

The Internet is run on computers called servers, such as these

Glossary

Air compressor a machine that compresses gases to create power.

Blackout turning off all lights, to deter enemy bombing in wartime.

Blueprint a detailed plan or outline.

Boar a kind of wild pig.

Carbon a chemical element.

Deciphering translating a secret code.

Engraving a form of printing created by cutting into wood or metal plate.

Excavated dug out of the ground.

Fertilizer animal manure or chemicals used to feed crops.

Flammable likely to catch fire.

Gas turbine a kind of engine that uses expanding gases to produce thrust.

Laboriously taking a lot of time and hard work.

Linen a type of cloth made from flax plants.

Morphine a substance extracted from opium poppies, which is addictive but can relieve pain and aid sleep.

Nutrient a source of food or nourishment.

Patent the exclusive right to make and use an invention.

Photographic negative an image captured on transparent paper that reverses lights and darks in a scene.

Piston part of an engine, consisting of a cylinder sliding inside a hollow cylinder.

Prototype the original model for a design.

Rotovator a machine for breaking up soil.

Sterilize to kill germs and bacteria.

Trench warfare fighting from deep trenches, as in World War I.

Turbo powered by rotating blades.

YouTube

Adam Sutherland

First published in 2014 by Wayland
Copyright © Wayland 2014

Wayland
338 Euston Road
London NW1 3BH

Wayland Australia
Level 17/207 Kent Street
Sydney, NSW 2000

Commissioning editor: Annabel Stones
Designer: LittleRedAnt (Anthony Hannant)
Picture researcher: Shelley Noronha

ISBN: 978 0 7502 8065 5
E-book ISBN: 978 0 7502 8530 8

Dewey categorisation: 338.7 61-dc23

Printed in Malaysia

10 9 8 7 6 5 4 3 2 1

Wayland is a division of Hachette Children's Books, an Hachette UK company.
www.hachette.co.uk

Picture acknowledgements: The author and publisher would like to thank the following
for allowing their pictures to be reproduced in this publication:
Cover: Eric Carr/Alamy; title page: IStock Images; p.4: Netphotos/Alamy; p.5: White House Photo/
Alamy; p.6: YouTube/Photoshot; p.7: Rex Features; p.8: UPPA/Photoshot; p.9: CTK/Alamy; p.11,
top: Shutterstock; p.11, bottom: AFP/Getty Images; p.12, top: Jeff Morgan 02/Alamy; p.12, bottom:
Picture Alliance/Photoshot; p.14: YouTube/Photoshot; p.15 WireImage/Getty; p.16 M91/CTK/Alamy;
p.17: Stefan Chabluk Illustration; p.18: Shutterstock; p.19: Shutterstock; p.20: AFP/Getty Images;
p.21: Paul Kitagaki Jr./Sacramento Bee/MCT/Photoshot; p.22 YouTube/Photoshot; p.23: YouTube/
Photoshot; p.24 Juliane Thiere/Alamy; p.25: Getty Images for YouTube; p.26: Photoshot; p.27
Keith Morris/Alamy.

2

Contents

It's a YouTube world

It's November 2013, and YouTube is streaming its first Music Awards live from New York City. With 60 million votes cast, and appearances on the night from global superstars Lady Gaga, Eminem and Taylor Swift, it could soon become as important an event in the music calendar as MTV's Video Music Awards. What next, a show to rival the Oscars?

YouTube's presence is all around us – and still growing. At the time of writing, the world's largest video streaming website attracts 800 million visitors every month, with over 72 hours of video uploaded every minute. By the time you read this, those figures will be even larger!

So how did the brainchild of three twentysomethings, launched from above a pizza restaurant in San Mateo, California, become not only the third most popular website in the world, but also such a unique source of entertainment, as well as an important social, and at times political, tool?

What started as a website for viral videos of singing cats is today believed to be the future of entertainment. Unlike television, YouTube allows you to watch what you want, when you want – finding content either through searches or social media recommendations.

YouTube was originally a source of cute, entertaining, user-generated content.

Just as importantly, YouTube channels have the ability to interact directly with their audience, take on board comments and tailor their content – practically in real time.

'The ability to interact with their audience is a critical part of [the channels'] success,' says Sara Mormino, director of YouTube content operations in Europe, the Middle East and Africa (EMEA). 'It's a two-way dialogue that was not possible with traditional media.'

Over the next pages, we look at the YouTube phenomenon – from its launch, growth, purchase by Google, and continued growth and huge financial losses – to the YouTube we know today. Enjoy the ride!

President Obama takes part in a online interview with YouTube from the White House in December 2012.

YouTube's march into the record books

Chad Hurley, 2006, Google press release on the purchase of YouTube

YouTube Today

800 Million+
monthly unique visitors
More than the total population of Europe

72 Hours+
video uploaded per minute
More than a decade of content every day

One Million+
partner program members
More than the total population of Delaware

No.2 Search Engine
Larger than Bing, Yahoo, Ask and AOL added together

Four Billion
hours of video viewed each month
More than 450,000 years of video every month

5

It's good to share

Ground-breaking ideas can often come from the simplest of sources. In the case of YouTube – the world's number one website for uploading, viewing and sharing videos – it began with a party for three workmates in San Francisco.

At the start of 2005, Chad Hurley, Steve Chen and Jawed Karim – all former employees of the secure web payment site Paypal – were having a dinner party. As the story goes, the trio were unable to find a way to quickly and simply share video clips after the event due to restrictions on the size of email attachments, and YouTube was born.

Chen has since commented that the birth of YouTube has been simplified 'for marketing purposes'. What we do know for sure is that the domain name www.youtube.com was activated on 14 February 2005 and the first video, a 19-second clip entitled 'Me at the zoo' featuring co-founder Jawed Karim, was uploaded on 23 April of the same year.

Jawed Karim at the zoo – YouTube's first ever clip!

The site was opened to the public in a 'beta' (testing) version in May 2005, six months before the official launch in November. The new company attracted investment of $3.5m (£2.1m) from venture capital firm Sequoia Capital. As well as money, they gained business expertise with Roelof Botha, former chief financial officer of Paypal, who joined the YouTube board of directors. In April 2006, Sequoia and fellow investment firm Artis Capital Management put a further $8m (£5m) into the business.

The money was spent on computing power – the huge network of servers that stores uploaded videos, and allows visitors to stream them smoothly and quickly. The site was a huge hit. By June 2006 more than 65,000 new videos were being uploaded, and the site was receiving 100 million video views every day.

Business Matters

Forming a company

A 'limited' or 'incorporated' company is a business owned by shareholders (people who own shares in the company), and run by directors. The company's shares have a basic value, for example £1 each, which stays the same, and a 'market value', which goes up and down depending on how good an investment the shares are judged to be by people outside the company who want to buy them.

Brains

Behind The Brand

Chad Hurley
YouTube co-founder and former CEO

As CEO of YouTube, Hurley oversaw the company's growth from a start-up to the world's third most visited website. Until he stepped down as CEO in October 2010, his role was overseeing the growth of the brand, and the transition into profit through advertising revenues.

Hurley has a BA in Fine Arts from Indiana University of Pennsylvania, and was hired as PayPal's first graphic designer. He created its official logo during his job interview!

In 2013, Hurley launched MixBit, a Smartphone video-editing app, with YouTube co-founder Steve Chen through their company AVOS Systems.

Along comes Google

Within a year of its launch, YouTube was ranked the fifth most popular site on the Internet. In the 12 months to August 2006, site visits had soared from 2.8 million to 72 million per month.

YouTube had become an Internet phenomenon. It was easy to use – you could watch videos on the site without downloading any special software, or even registering. And everything was there! If you wanted to see a clip of England winning the 1966 World Cup, or Lady Gaga wearing a dress made of meat at the Video Music Awards, they were both there, along with countless clips of weird, funny, informative and other cool stuff that site visitors loved.

> 66 The YouTube team has built an exciting and powerful media platform that complements Google's mission to organize the world's information and make it universally accessible and useful. 99
>
> *Google chief executive Eric Schmidt, 2006. Google press release on the purchase of YouTube.*

The Queen uploading a video to YouTube's Royal Channel in 2008, during a visit to Google HQ in London.

8

Business Matters

The Unique Selling Point (USP)

A USP is the unique quality about a company's product or service that will attract customers to use or buy it rather than an alternative product from a competitor. YouTube stood out from competitors because, according to co-founder Jawed Karim, it is a site 'where anyone could upload content that everyone else could view... Up until that point, it was always the people who owned the website who would provide the content'.

The Google empire, including YouTube, Chrome, Google + and Gmail.

In October, Google announced that it was buying YouTube for $1.65bn (£1.1bn).

Why? Advertisers love sites like YouTube that not only attract large amounts of traffic, but also have the potential to hold visitors for extended periods of time.

Google calculated that even if just 10 per cent of the $54bn (£33bn) spent annually on TV advertising made the shift to video sites like YouTube, then $1.65bn was a small price to pay for the income they could potentially earn.

According to Chad Hurley, YouTube decided to sell because they lacked the resources to cope with the site's extraordinary growth. 'When we started, we thought one million daily uploads would be great,' he remembers. Instead, they were getting a hundred times that many. 'We thought we'd burn up our bandwidth. We worried our servers would go down.'

At that time, YouTube was making no money, so the deal with Google meant financial investment, more servers and computers, more brainpower, and more help finding broadcast partners and figuring out how to place advertising on the site.

Millionaires overnight

Google's purchase of YouTube gave the owners shares in the search giant that were worth many millions of pounds!

Artis Capital Management $783m (£486m)

Sequoia Capital $446m (£277m)

Chad Hurley $395m (£245m)

Steve Chen $326m (£202m)

Jawed Karim $64m (£39m)

Content is king – as long as it's legal

By 2007 YouTube was becoming part of the mainstream – 7 of the 16 US Presidential candidates announced their campaigns on the site! It also set about gaining traditional broadcasters' confidence by tackling piracy and signing important content licensing deals.

Winning the support of the global entertainment industry was YouTube's biggest challenge. Many of its video clips were taken from films, TV shows or sporting events and uploaded to the site without the knowledge or permission of the broadcaster. Although YouTube offered to remove all offending videos when it received a complaint from the copyright holder, this was still a potential area of conflict – and costly lawsuits – that Google was keen to avoid.

YouTube and Google jointly announced a series of new distribution deals. Universal Music Group signed a deal protecting the rights of its label's artists, and US TV channel CBS signed a deal offering short video clips like news, sport and entertainment on the site. In turn, the CBS Videos YouTube channel earned CBS a share of advertising revenues.

YouTube also launched a content-management programme – Content ID – that alerted copyright holders automatically when any part of their content was uploaded. Copyright holders then had the option to remove it, sell ads against it, or use it as a promotional tool. Today, Content ID generates a third of YouTube's income.

In November 2008, YouTube signed further agreements with MGM, Lion's Gate and CBS, allowing all three to post full-length films and TV episodes on the site, accompanied by ads, in a section of the US website called 'Shows'. In November 2009, a version of 'Shows' was launched for UK viewers offering around 4,000 full-length shows from more than 60 partners.

The move helped YouTube keep growing in popularity. By 2010, it was ranked as the third most visited site on the Internet, behind Google and Facebook.

Business Matters

Branding

All the qualities and features of a product, including its name and its appearance, are presented to the customer as a brand. To be successful, all brands — from YouTube to McDonalds to Nike — need to be distinctive (stand out in some way from competitors), consistent (always provide the same level of quality, and therefore be seen as reliable), recognizable (through a logo or 'look' of a product) and attractive. The simple black and red YouTube logo has become as recognizable as a Nike swoosh or the McDonalds golden arches.

Brains

Behind The Brand

Steve Chen
co-founder of YouTube

Chen was born in Taiwan and moved to the USA with his family at eight years old. He studied computer science at the University of Illinois, but left before graduating to join PayPal as one of its first employees.

At YouTube, Chen was the company's chief technology officer. His role was to keep the site running smoothly, and quickly react to problems as they arose. Chen was a fellow employee of Chad Hurley's at PayPal, and helped PayPal launch in China. He is also a former employee of Facebook. He now co-owns AVOS Systems with Hurley.

YouTube's co-founders Chad Hurley and Steve Chen. The pair are still working together on new projects.

US Presidential candidates on stage in 2007, taking part in a debate broadcast live on YouTube.

YouTube in trouble

YouTube experienced huge growth and global brand awareness. It captured 43 per cent of the US online video market, and had 14 billion video views per month – but it still wasn't making money.

Advertisers, such as Hyundai, have increasingly turned to YouTube and away from traditional print media.

Two years into the program, YouTube was earning roughly $240m (£150m) in ad revenue. Unfortunately, its operating costs (computers, bandwidth, staff, office space and so on) cost an estimated $710m (£440m). That's a loss of over $470m (£290m)!

The problem was that there was far more user-generated content on the site than professionally produced material. This content was harder to monetize as advertisers prefer to run clips at the start of more popular films and TV shows. At the same time, this content added significantly to the costs of running the site, specifically in terms of bandwidth (the amount of computing power required to store the videos and stream them to site visitors).

In May 2007 YouTube launched its Partner Program, a system based on Google's AdSense advertising system, which allows the person who uploaded the video to share in the revenue produced by advertising on the site. YouTube takes 45% of the revenue with the other 55% going to the uploader.

YouTube's Partner Program has helped turn the slogan 'Broadcast Youself' into big money for many YouTubers.

YouTube had a number of choices: it could refocus the site on professionally produced content with existing customer loyalty and real monetization prospects, for example network TV shows; it could put its efforts into promotional partnerships with big-name brands like Nike, Toyota and Disney-Pixar; or it could adopt a subscription model, either charging people to view certain members-only content, or requiring users to create a paid account to be able to upload videos. All of these, however, were against the spirit of the site.

How would YouTube turn loss into profit, and keep its identity?

Brains

Behind The Brand

Jawed Karim
co-founder of YouTube

Karim was born in Germany but moved to the USA with his parents – both scientists – at 12 years old. Along with Steve Chen, he studied computer science at the University of Illinois but left before graduating to join PayPal. Much of PayPal's security software, including its anti-fraud protection, was designed by Karim.

When YouTube was sold to Google in 2006, Karim continued working part-time as an advisor, but went back to university to study computer science at Stanford University. In 2008, he launched a venture capital fund, Youniversity Ventures, to help students develop and launch their own businesses.

Profit and loss

A profit and loss statement is a company's financial report that indicates how the revenue (money received from the sale of products and services before expenses are taken out, also known as the 'top line') is transformed into the net income (the result after all revenues and expenses have been accounted for, also known as the 'bottom line'). It shows the revenues for a specific period, and the cost and expenses charged against those revenues. The purpose of the profit and loss statement is to show company managers and investors whether the company made or lost money during the period being reported.

The power of partners

...who had been Google's path to profit, and they were ...they could do the same for YouTube.

...first step was moving Salar Kamangar ...parent company Google over to YouTube. Kamangar had been one of the creator's of ...hugely profitable advertising system – ...advertisers for every thousand views ...(see ...).

...began to harness the power ...Partner Program to create a ...bedroom YouTube stars (see ...). By selling advertising on popular ...channels, the site generated ...revenue for its 30,000 partners. The ...500 partners now earn close to £100,000 per year!

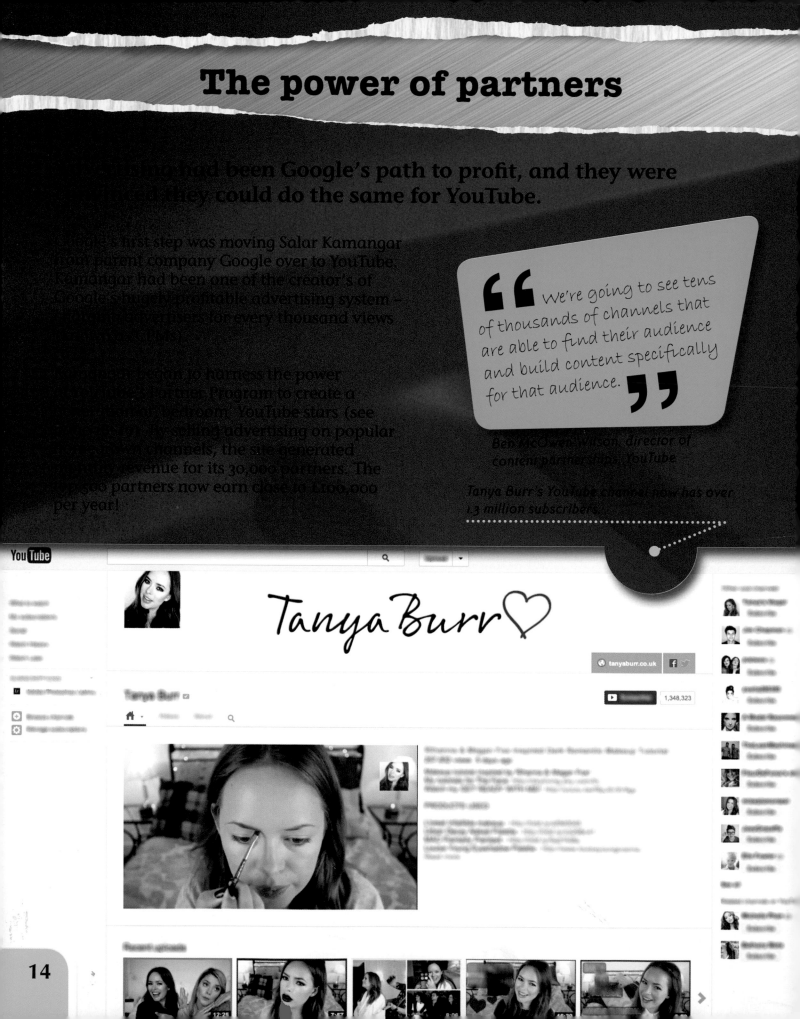

Next, Kamangar recruited Robert Kyncl (see biography on page 21). Kyncl pioneered web streaming of video at Netflix, striking deals with Hollywood studios to license its content online and generating huge profits for the company. At first, Kyncl concentrated on strengthening YouTube's own movie-streaming business. This met with limited success, however as many studios were already tied into long-term licensing deals with companies like Netflix.

Kyncl and Kamangar's next move was more ambitious: to turn YouTube into the world's number one resource for high-quality, studio-produced TV shows – 'webisodes' lasting between 4-10 minutes.

The idea was to recruit programme makers, offering $100m (£62m) in funding (advances against projected advertising revenues), and launching around 100 original channels. YouTube would have exclusive rights to stream the shows for one year, but apart from selling advertising, it would not invest in the promotion or marketing of the shows in the way that traditional TV channels do.

see biography on page 21

Three webisodes to watch now

WIGS
Short films and documentaries about the lives of women. Actress Anna Paquin from the *True Blood* series is one of the stars.
Average length: 7 mins
Subscribers: 257,000

All about the McKenzies
A British comedy likened to *The fresh prince of Bel Air*, with Samuel McKenzie dreaming of becoming a Hollywood acting legend.
Average length: 4 mins
Subscribers: 1,700

The Khan Academy
Offers 'a free world-class education for everyone'. Subjects include maths, computer programming and history.
Average length: 4 mins
Subscribers: 1.4m (million)

Skateboarder Tony Hawk now has his own YouTube channel, RIDE.

Among the 100 channels, notable examples were WIGS and The Khan Academy, the interactive comedy PBTV, skateboarder Tony Hawk's

YouTube goes global

Like its parent company Google, YouTube was focused on worldwide expansion, which opened up a massive global market of viewers – and advertisers.

In June 2007 Google CEO Eric Schmidt launched YouTube's new 'localization' system. Localization is a way of adapting computer software to specific regions or languages, for example the Basque dialect in France, or Catalan in Spain, by adding certain location-specific components, and translating text.

During June of that year, nine local YouTube channels launched, including Brazil, Japan, UK, Spain, France and Italy. Eight more followed before the end of the year,

including Australia, New Zealand, Canada (with English and French versions), Germany and Russia. By the end of August 2013, there were over 50 different language versions of the site, covering North and South America, Europe, the Middle East and Australasia.

The Czech language edition of YouTube, launched in October 2008.

The global expansion hugely increased YouTube's ability to generate advertising revenue through the site. Not only could large international brands now advertise on a global scale, but YouTube could also tap into lucrative national markets. In other words, viewers would always see advertising that was relevant to them whatever country they lived in.

However, YouTube's global reach has often been affected by censorship in certain countries, either on a temporary or permanent basis. At the time of writing, YouTube is permanently banned in China, Iran, Pakistan and Turkmenistan. More often, YouTube is banned temporarily if a country's government reacts angrily to content posted on the site.

For example, YouTube was banned in Libya in January 2010 when it featured videos of demonstrations by families of detainees killed in Abu Salim prison. It was reinstated at the end of 2011 after the Libyan Civil War.

Because of YouTube's global accessibility and massive number of users, its impact has grown from an entertainment site to a valuable tool in countries fighting for democracy. It can provide a broadcasting outlet for protest groups – a voice for people struggling to be heard. In that way, it is invaluable.

YouTube's global censorship

Business Matters

Expansion

This means increasing the size of a company, or the scale of its operations. In YouTube's case, this happened when they expanded beyond the US, so that eventually everyone in the world could use it. Expansion can make a business more profitable as well as more 'cost efficient', by increasing profits at a rate faster than costs.

- Tajikistan
- Afghanistan
- Turkmenistan
- Germany
- UK
- Russia
- Armenia
- Turkey
- Tunisia
- US
- Syria
- Iran
- China
- Morocco
- Bangladesh
- Libya
- Thailand
- Sudan
- UAE
- Pakistan
- Malaysia
- Indonesia
- Brazil

● Permanently blocked
● Temporarily blocked

YouTube superstars

The YouTube Partners Program has created a generation of YouTube superstars! Here we meet three of them.

Jamal Edwards, SB.TV
350,000 subscribers

At 14 years old, Londoner Jamal Edwards started recording videos of foxes raiding the dustbins outside the tower block where he lived. By 15 he was following the grime music scene, filming rappers performing for his Smokey Barz TV channel.

In 2009, Edwards persuaded YouTube to make him an official partner, and today the 22 year old has interviewed Prime Minister David Cameron, is credited by music artists Jessie J and Rita Ora as helping to launch their careers, and is worth an estimated £8m!

Edwards puts his success down to hard work and ambition. 'I was always trying to expand. I could have just stayed in West London, but [I went] east, north, south, central! I was uploading a video every day. I'd finish college, and I'd be editing my videos on the way home [to get] my clip online first.'

YouTuber Jamal Edwards at London Fashion Week 2013.

Tanya Burr
550,000 subscribers

Norfolk-born Burr left school at 16, did a short make-up course, and started work on the beauty counter of her local department store. When she got home, she would post step-by-step make-up tutorials on YouTube. 'Early on, they were mainly celebrities' looks,' she says. 'How to recreate famous faces.'

Two years later, Burr left her job to devote herself to her blog and tutorials full time. Like fellow YouTuber Zoella, Burr's influence over fans' buying habits has made her an important ally to fashion brands. A Mulberry handbag she featured in one video caused the Mulberry website to be bombarded with hits, and resulted in an invite for Burr to the Mulberry show at London Fashion Week. But Burr keeps her feet on the ground. 'The most important thing is to give viewers what they want and to keep the videos unique and professional.'

Charlie McDonnell, Charlieiscoollike
2.2m subscribers

McDonnell started posted videos from his home in Bath in April 2007 at the age of 16. One of his earliest videos 'How To Get Featured on YouTube' made it onto YouTube UK's homepage and saw his subscribers jump from 150 to 4,000 in just two days.

In January 2008, to celebrate reaching 25,000 subscribers he asked for challenge suggestions from viewers. He completed 25 videos, including a suggestion that came from TV presenter Philip Schofield and his daughter: to perform the 'Hoedown Throwdown' dance from the film *Hannah Montana: The Movie.*

In June 2011, McDonnell became the first UK YouTuber to reach one million subscribers. His videos now end with a voiceover from *QI* presenter Stephen Fry telling viewers they are honorary 'coollikes' for watching Charlie!

Behind the scenes at YouTube HQ

What's it like working at the heart of one of the most successful Internet companies in the world? We go behind the scenes at YouTube's California offices to find out.

Like the best companies in Silicon Valley, YouTube strives to find the very best talents and keep them from leaving. One way they do that is making employees' working lives as fun, entertaining and full of perks as possible.

If you're lucky enough to be one of the 550 employees working at YouTube's San Bruno headquarters, you can start your day by hopping onto one of the company's air-conditioned – and free – buses running in and out of San Francisco. Relax and forget about the rush hour traffic. In fact, bring your pet – many YouTubers bring their dogs to work with them every day.

When you arrive, grab a bike or a scooter – they're also provided free – and find your way to your desk. No gloomy workspaces here, everything is open-plan and well-designed with large windows to let in as much natural light as possible. In keeping with the green credentials, all work benches scattered around the office are made from eucalyptus grown on site.

The putting green at YouTube HQ – a good way to blow off steam!

At lunchtime, sit down for a healthy – and free! – lunch prepared by award-winning San Francisco chef Trent Page. If you're feeling a little drowsy on the way back to your desk, how about some downtime in one of the 'nap pods' spread around campus?

Business Matters

$

Human Resources

The Human Resources (HR) department of a company is responsible for putting in place and maintaining the business practices that allow effective people management. Some key responsibilities of an HR department are: 1) training; 2) staff appraisal: a formal process, performed by managers on their staff, which aims to communicate how they are performing and to discuss what they need in order to improve and develop; 3) staff development: the processes in the company designed to identify the people with potential, keep them in the organisation, and move them into the right positions.

Or if you're feeling more energetic, how about 15 minutes on the putting green – yes, it's inside the office, and a great spot for brainstorming!

In the afternoon, as you head to a meeting with co-workers in one of the conference rooms named after popular video games, don't bother with the lift, use the slide – in YouTube red – to quickly take you down from the third to the second floor.

Who said work can't be fun?

YouTube employees can take the slide between floors – in YouTube red of course.

Brains

Behind The Brand

Robert Kyncl
Global Head of Content

Czech Republic-born Kyncl oversees YouTube's business functions such as content, sales, marketing and operations. It is his job to extend YouTube into a specialized multi-channel environment.

Kyncl joined YouTube in 2010 from Netflix, where he was Vice President of Content Acquisitions and in charge of company acquisitions for streaming TV shows and movies over the Internet.

YouTube's greatest hits

What have been the most popular videos on YouTube? Here we list the ten most popular videos ever, and investigate landmarks in YouTube's video history.

A history in video

April 2005 YouTube co-founder Jawed Karim posts , 'Me at the zoo' – the first video on the site.

October 2005 Nike promotional video featuring footballer Ronaldinho is the first one million-hit clip.

December 2005 US comedy show *Saturday Night Live* airs 'Lazy Sunday' clip featuring comedian Andy Samberg, increasing YouTube traffic by 83%.

April 2006 'The Evolution of Dance', a 6-minute clip featuring 50 years of dance crazes, becomes the most popular clip in YouTube history with 131 million views.

May 2008 13 hours of video uploaded every minute.

January 2009 President Obama launches his own YouTube channel. The Pope launches his own YouTube channel. Live streaming of U2 concert.

March 2010 24 hours of video uploaded every minute.

April 2011 YouTube Live launches – providing live streaming of everything from the Royal wedding to the Olympics.

Feb 2013 72 hours of video uploaded every minute.

A clip from PSY's Gangnam Style – the video was a massive hit on YouTube.

From the first clip uploaded, Jawed Karim's 'Me at the zoo' (see page 6) to PSY's *Gangnam Style* – the most viewed video on YouTube, with over 1.7 billion views to date – YouTube has seen phenomenal growth. The growth has not just been in the amount of videos uploaded, and the number of people watching, but in the changing content from user-generated to mainstream music videos and network programming.

Business Matters

Critical mass

This is when a company expands until it achieves a strength or dominance in any particular market (or in YouTube's case, country) that means it achieves automatic brand recognition and can effectively control the market.

Brains
Behind The Brand

Salar Kamangar
CEO of YouTube

Kamangar replaced Chad Hurley as YouTube CEO in 2010. The ninth employee to join Google, Kamangar wrote the company's first business plan, and was responsible for its legal and financial departments, before becoming a founder member of its product team.

Before taking over at YouTube, Kamangar was Vice President of Google's Web Applications. He has a degree in Biological Sciences from Stanford University.

CEO Salar Kamangar has helped turn YouTube's loss into profit.

YouTube's ten most popular videos*

Rank	Video	Uploaded on	Number of views
1	Gangnam style by PSY	July 2012	
2	Baby by Justin Beiber	9 Feb 2010	
3	On the floor by Jennifer Lopez	3 March 2010	
4	Love the way you lie by Rihanna	5 Aug 2010	
5	'Charlie bit my finger – again!'	22 May 2007	
6	Party Rock Anthem by LMFAO	8 March 2011	
7	Gentleman by PSY	13 April 2013	
8	Waka Waka by Shakira	4 June 2010	
9	Bad Romance by Lady Gaga	23 Nov 2009	
10	Ai Se Eu Te Pego by Michel Teló	25 July 2011	

* Correct to October 2013

YouTube's political and social uses

In August 2013 chemical attacks on Syrian civilians left an estimated 1,400 people dead. British MPs were recalled from their summer break to view a report by the Joint Intelligence Committee, and decide what action to take in response to the attacks. As part of their decision process, they viewed a series of YouTube videos – watched over one million times – that formed the backbone of the report.

YouTube is no longer just an entertainment service. As we saw from the countries that censor YouTube (p16-17) the site's popularity and global reach means it is able to shine a light on everything from human rights abuses to homophobia and environmental concerns.

The 'It Gets Better' project was launched by US journalist Dan Savage in 2010. The YouTube channel tries to prevent suicides

among LGBT teenagers by conveying the message that these teens' lives will improve. The channel hosts over 50,000 videos, including many from celebrities, which have been viewed over 50 million times!

There is even a Human Rights Channel on YouTube, launched in 2012, which is a collaboration between the human rights organization WITNESS (www.witness.org) and social media news channel Storyful (www.storyful.com). The channel collects

Protest groups, like this member of the Anonymous, are able to speak directly to the public through videos on YouTube.

together and broadcasts videos shot by real people around the world who find themselves in extraordinary situations – from peace protesters coming under fire from government forces, to families caught up in guerrilla bombings. There are even 'How To' guides on filming protests, while staying safe.

YouTube is in a unique position – part of the mainstream, but also part of the underground. It allows news to be broadcast from countries where foreign journalists are not allowed; places where the real stories are often buried behind government restrictions and banning orders. As an eye on the real world, it is priceless.

Business Matters

Public relations (PR)

This is the practice of conveying messages to the public through the media on behalf of a client. The intention is to change the public's actions by influencing their opinions. For example, to view YouTube not just as an entertainment platform but also as a news delivery service. PR professionals usually target specific sections of the public ('audiences'), since similar opinions tend to be shared by a group of people rather than an entire society.

Brains

Behind The Brand

Danielle Tiedt
Head of Marketing

Tiedt was hired from Microsoft, where she spent 15 years, most recently as general manager of its Bing search engine. Her job was to try and get consumers to use a different search brand, and she oversaw an annual marketing budget of £74m!

At YouTube, Tiedt oversees the branding and promotion of the company's investment in new entertainment channels. It is her job to change users' perception of YouTube from fun web clips to professionally produced TV and movie-quality content.

Head of marketing, Danielle Tiedt, is helping change our views of YouTube.

What does the future hold for YouTube?

What are YouTube's plans for the next five years? Has it reached its peak or can it keep growing? Here we highlight some of the areas that YouTube may focus on to stay ahead of the competition.

We know for sure that YouTube will focus on creating more and more channels, broadcasting to smaller niche markets. Unlike traditional television, where airtime is limited, Internet 'airtime' is infinite. Quantity is just as important as quality, and YouTube relies on its audience choosing what they want to watch.

Advertising methods will need to change to target these niche markets. 'Currently it's one TV commercial run many times,' explains Robert Kyncl. 'It will become 250 video commercials run fewer times but to the right people, using geo-location, age-targeting and interest-targeting.' In other words, YouTube will be able to monitor what you watch, when you watch, how long you watch, and where you watch from – and deliver that information to advertisers, who in turn will show you advertising you actually want to see.

One challenge that YouTube faces is increasing the amount of time that people spend on the site. The average YouTuber currently spends around 5 hours per month on the site – a tiny amount compared to the 5 hours an average person spends watching television per day! If YouTube can persuade people to stay on the site longer, it can sell more advertising, and raise the rates it charges advertisers.

Longer shows would keep visitors on the site, and already there are examples of new shows, like the *Glee/High School Musical*-inspired drama *Side Effects* (produced by Awesomeness TV), running 40-minute episodes. YouTube has also tweaked its video-ranking algorithm to promote clips

Head of content, Robert Kyncl, is behind the successful YouTube Channels.

that keep viewers watching and engaged. So if a video leads to a person clicking on another video and spending more time on the site, it will rank higher.

One thing's for sure – YouTube will be a part of our lives for many years to come.

A group of university students watching YouTube. Will the site begin to rival traditional TV channels over the next 5-10 years?

Business Matters

Long-term success

Successful companies are 'market-driven', in other words they focus on satisfying the exact section of the market in which they operate. (All of YouTube's channels target specific markets, however niche.) Successful companies also need to be 'sustainable', meaning that people not only want to use their services now, but that they will continue to want to use them in the future.

YouTube's competitors – and how they measure up

www.metacafe.com
Simply designed site offering music, movies, games, and a variety of channels from Video Game High School to Annoying Orange that are also available on YouTube.

www.Dailymotion.com
Cluttered but very popular site attracting 112 million monthly visitors. Users can open accounts and interact with others.

www.vimeo.com
Stylishly designed site with an active community of users. Charges between £37-£125 per year for video uploads over a certain volume per year.

www.veoh.com
Small but well organized video-sharing site owned by Israeli start-up Qlipso, focuses more on online community than the quality/uniqueness of its videos.

27

Invent the next YouTube channel!

To create a new product, for example a new YouTube channel, it is helpful to produce a product development brief like the one below. This is a sample brief for a new YouTube channel called Football 24/7.

The SWOT analysis on the page opposite will help you to think about the strengths, weaknesses, opportunities and threats for your product. This can help you to see how feasible and practical your idea is before you think of investing time and money in it.

Product Development Brief

Name of channel: Football 24/7

Type of channel: Bringing the best streamed coverage of football matches from around the world – both new and classic archived games from the last 50 years.

The channel explained (use 25 words or less): Football 24/7 gives you access to the best live football from around the world, with a massive archive of classic matches too!

Target age of users: Users must be 16 and over to subscribe.

What does the channel do?: Football 24/7 allows viewers to access a huge archive of matches from around the world – from live games to classic matches. If you want to watch your heroes – from Diego Maradona to Cristiano Ronaldo – Football 24/7 is the one-stop channel for all football fans.

Are there any similar products already available?: None that we are aware of.

What makes your brand different?: Sky and BT offer Premier League and international live games, but no channel offers such a range of classic matches from around the world to enjoy in full at any time.

SWOT Analysis
(Strengths, Weaknesses, Opportunities and Threats)

Name of YouTube channel you are assessing ...
Football 24/7

The table below will help you assess your YouTube channel. By addressing all four areas, you can make your product stronger and more likely to be a success.

Questions to consider

Strengths

Does your channel offer something unique?
Is there anything innovative about it?
What are its USPs (unique selling points)?
Why will people use this channel instead of a similar one?

There are no other channels currently available offering the same service.

Football 24/7's USP is that it's the only place you can stream full matches from around the world from the last 50 years.

Weaknesses

Why wouldn't people use this channel?
Can everyone use it?
Does it does everything it says it can?

Football 24/7 is only of interest to football fans. Plus it will mostly appeal to older fans, who want to reminisce over games they might have seen, or heard about from many years ago.

Users have to be over 16 to subscribe to the channel.

At first the archive of older games will be limited, but more will come online all the time, as licensing deals are signed with international broadcasters for their archives

Opportunities

Will the area that the channel serves become more important over time?
Can the channel be improved in the future, e.g. adapted for other uses?
Can it be used globally?
Can it develop new USPs?

We predict that around the time of big tournaments, e.g. World Cups and European Championships, the demand for the channel will increase.

If the channel is a success, it could be expanded to cover other sports, e.g. American football and Cricket.

The channel could also expand to include interviews and programmes about classic players.

Threats

Is the market that you are selling into shrinking?
Will it face competition from other channels?
Are any of your weaknesses so bad they might affect the channel in the long run?

The popularity of football worldwide is increasing – no danger of the market reducing.

Other broadcasters with large archives of their own, e.g. the BBC and Sky, may not licence content to Football 24/7 and decide to launch their own channels instead.

We believe that the opportunities to generate revenue from advertising on the clips will persuade content providers to licence us their content.

Do you have what it takes to work at YouTube?
Try this quiz!

1) You're going to a friend's birthday party tonight. Do you:

a) Worry about what to buy her for a present. Then stick a tenner in an envelope.

b) Remind yourself to take some pictures to post on Facebook afterwards.

c) Video everything – from getting ready to the moment she blows out the candles – and post it for all your friends!

2) You have a presentation to do at school. Do you:

a) Find out what your best friend's writing about and do the same thing.

b) Spend a couple of nights on it, then print out some pictures from the Internet to liven it up.

c) Edit a video of clips you have found online.

3) You want to learn the guitar. Do you:

a) Buy a book of 'Easy Beatles songs' – then give up after page 10.

b) Go to a guitar teacher for a few weeks, but stop because you can't afford the cost of lessons any more.

c) Teach yourself from videos. There are some amazing teachers online, and all free!

4) What do you want to do when you leave school?

a) I'm hoping to work for my dad. Then I can be late for work, and he won't sack me.

b) University first. Then a job in banking.

c) I want to study computer science, then get a job with a start-up. I love social media!

5) Your hero is:

a) Jack Whitehall – a great stand-up comedian.

b) Nelson Mandela – led South Africa out of apartheird.

c) Chad Hurley – founder of YouTube.

6) You have the chance to meet one YouTuber. Who would it be?

a) Charlie –from 'Charlie bit my finger – again!'

b) PSY from *Gangnam Style* – I want to learn his dance moves.

c) Jamal Edwards – the opportunity to get any tips from him would be amazing!

7) You have the opportunity to launch your own YouTube channel. Do you:

a) Ask a few friends for ideas... and then forget about it.

b) Launch a channel with videos of your cat sleeping. Then be disappointed when it only gets 20 views.

c) Choose a subject that you really enjoy. And most importantly, be original, be funny, and upload regularly!

Results

Mostly As: Sorry, but your chance of working at YouTube is looking shaky! It doesn't sound like you have the interest in video streaming or social media to succeed at this world-famous company.

Mostly Bs: You are thoughtful and hard-working, but you need to put more effort into standing out from the pack if you want to succeed in a very competitive business.

Mostly Cs: Congratulations, it sounds like you have what it takes to succeed at YouTube. Keep working hard at school, and pushing to be the best, and who knows?

Glossary

algorithm a set of mathematical instructions that a computer uses to help calculate an answer or mathematical problem

bandwidth a measurement of the amount of information that can be sent between computers through a phone line

brainchild an original idea, plan or object that someone has invented

brainstorming meeting to suggest new ideas for possible development

censor to remove anything offensive from books, films and so on

copyright holder the person or organization who holds the legal right to control the production, distribution or selling of a film, photograph, piece of music or similar

eucalyptus a type of tree

harness to control something (in order to use its power)

homophobia a fear or dislike of gay people

LBGT lesbian, gay, bisexual and transgender

lucrative producing a lot of money

mainstream considered normal by most people

monetize to convert something into a form of currency

niche market a small area of trade within the economy, usually involving specialist interests

perception a belief or opinion, often held by many people

phenomenal extremely successful, especially in a surprising way

post upload to the Internet

scale to increase the size and importance of a company

streaming sending audio or video to a computer or mobile phone directly from the Internet, so that it doesn't need to be downloaded and saved first

tailor to make something specially, so that it is right for a particular person or group

unique unusual, or one of a kind

venture capital money lent to someone to start a new business, especially one that involves risks and will make large profits if successful

viral becoming popular very quickly through communication from one person to another on the Internet

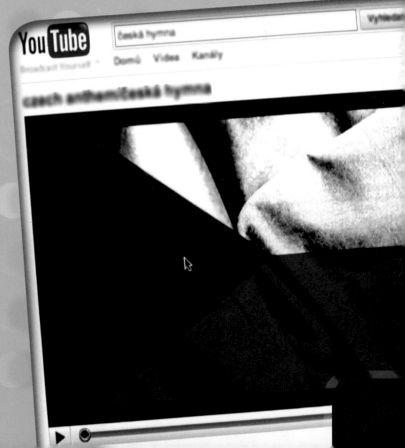

Index

BIG BU$INE$$

Contents of titles in this series:

More titles in the Big Business series

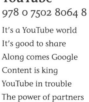

WAYLAND

THE ANCIENT ROMANS
Their Lives and Their World

PAUL ROBERTS

THE BRITISH MUSEUM PRESS

© 2009 Paul Roberts

Published in 2009 by British Museum Press
A division of The British Museum Company Ltd
38 Russell Square, London WC1B 3QQ

ISBN 978 0 7141 3127 6

Paul Roberts has asserted his right to be
identified as the author of this work

A catalogue record for this title is available
from the British Library

Designed and typeset by John Hawkins
Cover design by Jim Stanton
Printed in China by C&C Offset Printing Co. Ltd.

Illustration Acknowledgements

Unless otherwise noted below, the photographs in this book
show objects from the collections of the British Museum.
They were taken by the Photographic and Imaging
Department of the British Museum and are
© The Trustees of the British Museum.

Akg-images/Erich Lessing: 25 top right, 33 bottom right

© The Ancient Art and Architecture Collection: 55 top right,
66 top left

© The Art Archive/Gianni Dagli Orti: 59 bottom right.

© Corbis/Sygma: 72 bottom

© Foto Scala, Firenze: 55 bottom right

© Institute of Nautical Archaeology: 57 top left

© Phoenix Art Museum, Arizona, USA/The Bridgeman Art
Library: 76 bottom

© RMN/Konstantinos Ignatiadis: 51 right

© Paul Roberts: 9 bottom right, 10 bottom left, 15 right, 22
bottom right, 28 left, 38 centre right, 54 bottom left, 57
bottom, 58 top right, 59 bottom left, 61 bottom left, 65 top
right, 71 bottom right

© Walters Art Museum: 74–5

CONTENTS

INTRODUCTION

The city of Rome ruled over one of the greatest empires the world has ever seen. For almost five hundred years the Roman empire united all the countries round the Mediterranean Sea and much of Europe, from Spain to Syria and from Britain to Egypt.

Rome had a very strong army, which conquered new lands and guarded the existing empire. And what an incredible empire it was! A network of cities was linked by thousands of miles of well-built roads. The cities teemed with people from all over the world. They were filled with colonnaded piazzas, grand public buildings such as baths, temples and theatres and rich, beautifully decorated houses. An army of slaves and servants did everything from cleaning the streets to running shops and businesses and keeping the public baths heated.

A cameo portrait of the emperor Augustus.

A bronze model of a racing chariot.

Some parts of Rome had crowded high-rise apartment slums where the poor people lived. Noisy, smelly markets, crowded streets and the bustling city-centre Forum were filled with shops and stalls selling food, drink, consumer goods and luxuries from all over Italy and the empire. Many of the shopkeepers were women. Women were very important and very visible in everyday life, and in some ways were almost equal to men. And there were lots of children. Very many children died young because of germs and disease, so Romans tried to have big families to make sure some of them survived.

A marble portrait of a young boy.

The Roman empire ended more than 1500 years ago but it isn't forgotten. In the western world, our languages, literature, religion, architecture, laws and even the position and shape of our cities have all been influenced by Rome. Books, television and films tell us about Rome and Pompeii, gladiators and emperors. This book uses objects from the collections of the British Museum, together with pictures of Rome and other cities, to introduce you to the people of this amazing empire.

The Roman gods controlled everything. Priests and priestesses served the gods faithfully, often for most of their lives. Religious festivals were important, but they were also the time for people to relax and enjoy themselves, often by watching 'the games'. There were no organized team games, like today's cricket and football. Instead there were chariot races, beast fights and gladiator combats.

Romans also liked the theatre, where they could watch sad or funny plays. Actors, charioteers and gladiators were like today's rock stars, TV celebrities and film stars all rolled into one!

Painted portrait of a woman from Roman Egypt.

A bronze figure of a Roman legionary soldier.

MAP OF THE ROMAN EMPIRE

*Map of the Roman empire at its largest extent,
in around AD 117.*

TIMELINE

2000–1000 BC	The first farming villages are built near the river Tiber, in the area that will later become the city of Rome.
753 BC	Mythological date that Romulus founds Rome.
753–509 BC	Seven kings rule Rome.
509 BC	Tarquin the Proud, the last king of Rome, is expelled from the city. The Roman Republic begins.
264–202 BC	Rome fights three wars against Carthage, the north African city that ruled the western Mediterranean.
200 BC	Rome defeats the Carthaginian general Hannibal and conquers all of Italy.
146 BC	Rome destroys Carthage and Corinth, the capital of Greece. Rome now rules the Mediterranean.
55–54 BC	Julius Caesar leads military expeditions to Britain.
44 BC	Julius Caesar is killed by Romans who fear he is taking too much power. The Roman republic ends.
27 BC	Octavian becomes Augustus, the first emperor. The Roman empire begins.
AD 64	The Great Fire of Rome.
AD 79	The cities of Pompeii and Herculaneum are destroyed by the eruption of Mount Vesuvius.
AD 80	The Colosseum is completed.
AD 117	Hadrian becomes emperor after Trajan's death. The empire is at its largest extent.
AD 213	Caracalla declares every free person in the empire to be a citizen.
AD 313	The emperor Constantine legalizes Christianity.
AD 330	Constantine builds a new Christian capital at Constantinople (Istanbul).
AD 391	Theodosius closes all pagan temples.
AD 395	The empire officially splits between east and west.
AD 410	Rome is burnt by the barbarians.
AD 476	The western Roman empire falls. Romulus Augustulus, the last western Roman emperor, is sent into exile.
AD 1453	Constantinople is captured by the Ottoman Turks. End of the eastern Roman empire.

1 KINGS

At first, Rome was ruled by kings. Some of these kings are known only through stories. Romans thought their first king was Romulus. Romulus was abandoned with his twin brother Remus near the Palatine Hill in Rome, and a she-wolf raised them.

> A she-wolf making her way down for a drink heard crying and found the babies in their basket. A shepherd came by and found her feeding them and licking their faces.
>
> Livy

A burial vase, in the shape of an early Roman house.

Silver coin showing the she-wolf with Romulus and Remus.

When they grew up, Romulus killed Remus and ruled as Rome's first king. Archaeologists have found traces of villages from that period, so there might be some truth in the legend. The village houses were very simple – not the grand buildings we usually think of in Rome.

SEVEN KINGS

For about two hundred and fifty years, 753–509 BC, seven kings ruled Rome. They built the structure of Roman society. Romulus created the assembly of the people and the senate, a council of rich aristocrats. But Rome needed more people, so Romulus made it an asylum, a refuge for runaways – even criminals. He also kidnapped all the women from a nearby tribe, the Sabines! But later, the Romans and Sabines agreed to be friends.

The kings gradually captured more land and increased Rome's power and influence.

THE END OF THE KINGDOM

The last three kings were all Etruscans, from north of Rome. They made Rome a proper, united city. Tarquin drained marshy areas, created the first big city centre, the Forum Romanum, and built the Circus Maximus for chariot racing. Servius Tullius surrounded all seven of the city's hills with walls for the first time. The last king was another Tarquin, nicknamed 'the proud'. He built the enormous temple of Jupiter Optimus Maximus on the Capitoline Hill.

But Tarquin II was also a cruel king. The Romans became so angry at his bad behaviour that in 509 BC they finally threw him out of the city. The kingdom of Rome was over.

Statue of king Servius Tullius.

SVBLATO FRATRE ROMVLVS INITIA VRBIS LOCAT EAMQ ASVE NOMINE APPELLAT ROMAM

Romulus supervises the building of his new city. This print was made in around 1573.

2 SENATORS AND GENERALS

After the last Etruscan king was thrown out in 509 BC, Rome became a republic. It was supposed to be ruled by the people, but power really belonged to the senate, a council of six hundred rich and powerful men.

Below the senators were the consuls, who were meant to be replacements for the kings. There were always two so that one man couldn't have all the power. Then came the knights, less wealthy than the senators but still important, and finally the ordinary people, or plebeians.

The Curia or Senate House in the Roman Forum.

Officials called lictors went everywhere with the consuls. They carried a fasces, a bundle of sticks with an axe. It meant a consul could beat you (or kill you!).

WAR AND CONQUEST

Rome had to defend herself against powerful enemies. When the last king tried to recapture Rome, one man, Horatius, single-handedly defended the wooden bridge that led into the city.

> 'You must destroy the bridge, cut it down, burn it. I'll hold the Etruscans off as best I can.' He stood there firmly on the bridge ... then there was a crash of splintering wood. Fully armed, Horatius jumped into the river Tiber. Spears flew thick around him, but he swam to his own side unharmed.
>
> Livy

In 390 BC the heroes were birds! Rome was attacked and burnt by Celts from northern Europe. The last fortress, the Capitol Hill, was about to be taken when the sacred geese of the temple of Juno, queen of the gods, started to cackle and honk. This woke up the Roman guards and the city was saved.

Over the next two hundred years Rome conquered the rest of Italy. Then she started to conquer all the countries around the Mediterranean sea. Rome defeated generals such as Hannibal, who brought his army (with elephants) from north Africa into Italy.

Elephant-shaped vase, used for pouring olive oil.

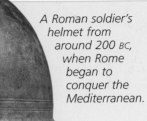

A Roman soldier's helmet from around 200 BC, when Rome began to conquer the Mediterranean.

As Rome's power grew, gold, jewels and slaves flooded into the city, especially from Greece. Rome changed for ever. People became rich. They built beautiful temples and houses, filled with statues, mosaics and paintings. But all this money caused arguments between senators, generals and the ordinary people.

Iron ring with a gold portrait of Julius Caesar.

Civil wars broke out and the republic began to crumble. Famous generals such as Pompey and Julius Caesar tried to save it.

Caesar stopped the civil wars by declaring himself a 'dictator'. But people thought he wanted to make himself a king so he was assassinated on the Ides of March (15 March), 44 BC. The republic was over.

> The assassins closed in a circle around Caesar. Wherever Caesar turned, he met daggers. Like a wild animal in a trap, he received twenty-three stab wounds.
>
> Plutarch

3 EMPERORS

The Roman republic was officially ruled by the senate and the people, but there were others who held positions of power in Rome, including consuls, generals, and chief priests. When Augustus became the first emperor in 27 BC, he was given (or took) all the top jobs for himself. This made him, and the emperors after him, the most powerful men in the world.

Some emperors were loved by the people, for example Augustus, the founder of the empire, or the soldier emperors Vespasian and Trajan. Others, like Caligula, Nero or Domitian, were described by the Roman writers as monsters, or as very strange:

> Early in his reign he spent a lot of time catching flies and stabbing them with a sharp pen.
>
> Suetonius, describing the emperor Domitian

Bronze head of Augustus, the first emperor of Rome.

WHAT EMPERORS DID

Every emperor, good or bad, had the same powers.
He was head of state (*princeps*), head of the state
religion (*pontifex maximus*) and head of the armed
forces (*imperator*). *Imperator* – commander in chief –
gives us our word 'emperor'. The emperor's family also
had important roles in Roman society. Augustus's wife
Livia and later empresses were very involved in politics,
and the children of the imperial family were adored by
the ordinary people.

POWER AND PUBLICITY

Each emperor needed to show the empire how
powerful he was, and what he looked like. He had no
television, internet or newspapers, so all over the empire
he set up thousands of bronze and stone statues of
himself and his family. Millions of coins carried his
profile and people wore the
emperor's portrait on
jewellery such
as rings, carved
stone cameos
or necklaces.

Marble head of the emperor Vespasian.
He helped conquer Britain, and built the
Colosseum.

A rare gemstone portrait
of Claudius, the emperor
who invaded Britain.

NERO

Nero was the last of Augustus's family to be emperor. He liked to drive racing chariots and to write and perform poetry and music. At the beginning of Nero's reign the people loved him. But he changed. His behaviour became unpredictable and violent. He killed both his wives as well as his own mother, Agrippina.

Marble head of the emperor Nero.

She survived a shipwreck (organized by Nero) but was then murdered by her son's troops. When the Great Fire of Rome devastated the city in AD 64, Nero blamed the Christians, and murdered hundreds of them in horrible ways.

Nero took a large area of the burnt-out city centre and built himself a huge palace, the Golden House (Domus Aurea).

Head of Agrippina.

It was filled with beautiful mosaics, sculptures and wall-paintings.

> Every inch of the house was covered with gold and jewels. Dining rooms had ivory ceilings with openings to shower guests with flowers and perfume. The ceiling of the banqueting hall revolved just like the sky.
>
> Suetonius

and when Nero moved in he said,

> 'At last I can live like a human being'.

But Nero made too many enemies, and he was forced to commit suicide. He stabbed himself in the neck with a dagger, saying 'What a great artist I was!'

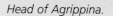

Fragment of painted decoration from Nero's Golden House.

HEAD OF STATE

As *princeps* (head of state) the emperor personally organized the administration of Rome and the empire. He sat in the senate house, listening to debates and passing new laws. He judged court cases, chose governors for Rome's provinces and generals for her armies. He even controlled Rome's fire brigade! People sent letters or visited the palace asking the emperor for his help and advice.

In about AD 100 the Roman writer Pliny, who was governor of one of the eastern provinces of the empire, asked the emperor Trajan how to deal with Christians. Trajan replied fairly, 'punish them if they have really done wrong, but don't hunt them down'.

Bust of the emperor Trajan.

IMPERIAL BUILDINGS

The emperor was also the major patron of building in Rome. Augustus rebuilt so much of the city in rich imperial style – the Forum, theatres and temples – that he said:

> 'I found Rome a city of brick and left it a city of marble'.

The ruins of the Baths of Caracalla.

Later emperors did the same. Vespasian and his son Titus built the enormous Colosseum for beast hunts and gladiator fights and Caracalla and Diocletian built enormous public baths (*thermae*).

Not just in Rome, but all over the empire, emperors paid for buildings, roads and bridges to show how rich, generous and powerful they were.

> The emperor Trajan had this road built by cutting through mountains and eliminating the bends.
> From a milestone near the River Danube, AD 100.

HADRIAN

When Hadrian became emperor in AD 117 he decided not to conquer more territory. Instead, he strengthened and fortified the empire by building defences, such as Hadrian's Wall in Britain. He wanted to see the empire's needs and problems, so he spent about ten years of his reign travelling round it. He was very well educated, and he loved Greek language and culture. He even wore a beard – a Greek fashion – and was the first emperor to do so. Some people thought he was too fond of Greek things, and nicknamed him *Graeculus* - 'that little Greek'.

Hadrian was a keen architect, and he helped design many important buildings in Rome, including the Pantheon, and his own tomb, now the Castel Sant'Angelo. He also rebuilt complete cities, such as Cyrene in Cyrenaica (modern Libya) and Athens in Greece.

At Tivoli, near Rome, he built himself a huge villa, even bigger and more beautiful than the imperial palace.

Bust of Hadrian.

Hadrian's Wall in northern Britain.

The Pantheon in Rome.

HEAD OF THE STATE RELIGION

As *pontifex maximus* (high priest) the emperor was head of the Roman state religion, with its many gods. The most important part of this religion was the sacrificing of animals. The emperor made sure that everything was done correctly and led the citizens in prayer.

Bust of Marcus Aurelius, dressed as a priest.

LIVIA – THE POWER BEHIND THE THRONE

The empress Livia was a very powerful, clever woman. She and Augustus were married for over fifty years.

Coin of Livia from a Greek city. The writing calls her 'goddess and Augusta'.

Livia wanted Tiberius, her son from her first marriage, to be emperor after Augustus, but there were several other candidates. Mysteriously, all of them died, and some people said that Livia knew all about it. She wanted her power to last for ever, and to be worshipped as divine. Augustus wouldn't allow it in Rome, but in other parts of the empire Livia got her wish. Statues showed her as part woman, part goddess.

Head of Livia, looking like the goddess Ceres.

HEAD OF THE ARMY

As *imperator* (commander in chief) the emperor was the supreme head of the armed forces and soldiers and sailors swore an oath of loyalty to him. Some emperors expanded the empire. This brought in more money, territory and slaves, and it made the emperor look even more powerful. Emperors such as Augustus and Trajan sometimes led the army themselves and spent years away from Rome on campaign.

A victorious emperor returned to Rome and celebrated a 'triumph'. A triumph was a great procession starring the emperor, his face painted red to look like a god. It passed through the Forum, displaying slaves and treasure captured in the campaign. Emperors built monuments such as arches and columns to celebrate their victories. But some emperors never returned from their campaigns. Septimius Severus died in AD 211 at York in northern Britain, after fighting the tribes of Caledonia (modern Scotland).

Statue of Septimius Severus as imperator.

Pottery plaque showing captives during a triumph.

UNHAPPY ENDINGS?

Emperors had complete control of the empire and all its people. They had their palaces, bodyguards and enormous amounts of money. But Roman writers (as far as they can be trusted!) tell us that emperors rarely died happily.

Tiberius, Augustus's stepson and successor, was smothered with a pillow by his chief bodyguard. The next emperor, Caligula (who was probably involved in Tiberius' death), was assassinated during a theatre performance. Caligula's uncle Claudius, who followed him, was poisoned by Agrippina, his own wife.

Her son Nero, the emperor after Claudius, became so unpopular that he was forced to commit suicide. Even the great Augustus, the first emperor, was probably killed by poisoned figs – possibly served by his own wife Livia!

Tiberius, who was murdered in his luxurious palace on the island of Capri, near Naples.

Cameo showing the emperor Augustus as a god, after his death.

Vespasian managed to joke about dying: 'Oh heavens, I think I'm becoming a god.'

4 GODS AND GODDESSES

Rome had many gods and goddesses, and each one had control over a different area of daily life. The twelve gods of the state religion were the most important. They were very like the twelve Greek Olympian gods, but they had different names and sometimes different responsibilities. Three of them were especially important. Jupiter (Greek *Zeus*) was the king of the gods. His queen Juno (Greek *Hera*) was the protector of women, especially in childbirth. Their daughter Minerva (Greek *Athena*) was the goddess of arts, crafts and knowledge. These were the three main gods of Rome and they were worshipped in the Temple of Jupiter on the Capitoline Hill. Venus (Greek *Aphrodite*), goddess of love, beauty and fertility, was believed to be the ancestor of Romulus, the founder of Rome. Julius Caesar said he was descended from the goddess too.

> Julius Caesar built the temple to his ancestor Venus Generitrix ... inside he put a beautiful statue of his lover Cleopatra – it's still there.
>
> Appian

Bronze statuette of Jupiter, the king of the gods.

Marble statue of
Venus, the goddess
of love and beauty.

Bronze statuette
of Cerberus,
Pluto's three-
headed dog,
who guarded
the Underworld.

The other major gods were Apollo (Greek *Apollo*), god of the sun, light and music, Mars (Greek *Ares*), god of war, Bacchus (Greek *Dionysos*), god of wine and fertility, Ceres (Greek *Demeter*), the goddess of corn and agriculture, Vesta (Greek *Hestia*) the goddess of the hearth and home, Neptune (Greek *Poseidon*), god of the sea, Pluto (Greek *Hades*) god of the underworld, and Vulcan (Greek *Hephaistos*), god of fire and volcanoes.

Terracotta bust
of Bacchus, the
god of wine
and fertility.

Marble statue of Apollo with
a lyre (a stringed instrument)
and his sacred snake.

THE MINOR GODS

Some gods were linked to the countryside, including Pomona, the goddess of fruit, Faunus (Greek *Pan*), the god of woods and wild land, and Lupercus the god of shepherds and flocks. One of the most unusual gods was Robigo, the god of mould and failed crops – farmers prayed to him to stay away!

There were also demigods or heroes, who were half-human and half-god, such as Hercules (Greek *Herakles*). Hercules was worshipped because people believed he was a bridge between humans and gods. The twelve tasks, or labours, of Hercules were very popular in Roman art and mythology.

Bronze statuette of Hercules. He has just taken the golden apples – one of his twelve tasks.

Stone cameo showing two royal princesses as goddesses.

EMPEROR-WORSHIP

During the empire an important part of Roman religion was emperor-worship. People began to worship the emperors and their families as living gods.

Augustus didn't like the idea of this in the city of Rome itself, but allowed it in the other parts of the empire. Temples were set up for emperor-worship, and statues and beautiful jewellery showed the emperor and his family with the faces or the clothing of the gods. After emperors died they were made into gods (deified) by a decree of the senate.

The temple of the deified emperor Antoninus Pius and his wife Faustina in the Forum in Rome.

DOMESTIC WORSHIP

Religion was not always so grand. Ordinary people had shrines to the gods in their own homes and on the street corners of their neighbourhoods. People made simple offerings of chickens, small animals, or wine. To ordinary people this domestic worship was very important. Most Roman houses had a shrine for the *Lares*, the spirits of their ancestors, called a *lararium*. The *Lares* and *Penates*, the patron gods of the family, guarded the house and everyone in it.

Bronze statuette of a lar, a household spirit.

FOREIGN GODS

The empire grew to a huge size and the many different peoples conquered by Rome had their own gods and goddesses. The Romans usually let conquered peoples go on worshipping their own gods, and even adopted foreign gods into Roman religion. For example, the strange mystical cult of the eastern goddess Cybele, the Great mother, came to Rome from the part of Asia now called Turkey.

A legend said that Asclepius, the god of medicine and healing, came to Rome from Greece because the Romans prayed to him to rescue them from a terrible plague.

Men who had served in the army, immigrants and slaves brought other important gods to Rome. The worship of the goddess Isis and her husband Serapis came from Egypt. Temples were built to her all over the empire. In Rome she had a huge temple in the centre of the city. At Pompeii her temple was beautifully decorated with paintings showing her festivals and ceremonies.

ΑΣΚΛΗ
ΠΙΩ
ΚΑΙ
ΥΓΕΙΑ
ΤΥΧΗ
ΕΥΧΑΡΙΣ
ΤΗΡΙΟΝ

Stone relief thanking Asclepius and his daughter Hygeia for helping to heal a bad leg.

Statue of the Egyptian goddess Isis.

NEW RELIGIONS

In the third century AD the empire was in political and military trouble. Many people stopped believing in the old gods and turned to religions that promised them a better life after they died. They often converted to religions that had only one god – they were *monotheist* (from the Greek words 'one god'). Some chose Mithras, a god originally from Persia (modern Iran).

Mithraism was particularly popular with the army, because just as in the army, a follower of Mithras could be promoted through the ranks. He started off as a beginner, called a soldier (*miles*) but could reach the highest level, called father (*pater*).

People also started worshipping the sun god Sol or Phoebus and around AD 220 the emperor Heliogabalus built a huge temple to Sol in Rome.

Silver disk showing the sun-god Sol in his chariot.

Marble statue of the eastern god Mithras and a bull.

Monotheism was not new. The Jews had worshipped their one god for many centuries, but the most successful monotheist religion was Christianity. After the death of Christ in about AD 35 the new religion spread quickly, especially amongst the poor. Christianity promised a better life after death, and it included everyone, even women and slaves. Some emperors, like Nero, persecuted Christians because they would not sacrifice to the emperor and the empire.

Thousands of Christians were killed in the racing circus or the arena.

In AD 313 the emperor Constantine issued an imperial proclamation that gave equal rights to the Christians.

Christians became very powerful and eventually the emperors themselves became Christian. In AD 391 Theodosius made Christianity the state religion and closed the temples of the pagan gods and heroes for ever.

Mosaic from Hinton St Mary in England showing Christ.

Marble head of the emperor Constantius, who allowed Christians to worship freely.

5 PRIESTS AND PRIESTESSES

The many gods and goddesses of Rome had to be looked after and kept happy so that they would protect Rome and keep the empire, the emperor and the people safe. Festivals and sacrifices had to be organized, and there was an army of priests and priestesses to do this.

> Oh Jupiter the Best and Greatest, we sacrifice to you this splendid bull as it is written in the holy books so that good fortune may come to the Roman people.
>
> An inscription from Rome

Bronze head of a young priest. The band around his head shows his status as a holy man.

SACRIFICES TO THE GODS

The Romans consulted the gods before beginning any important project – declaring war, putting up a new building, making a journey, getting married or having children. If you wanted to consult the gods you had to give them presents, called offerings or sacrifices. People sometimes made libations, liquid offerings of wine, milk or honey. They also burnt fragrant incense on the gods' altars. But the most important offering was the sacrifice of living animals.

Sacrifices took place at the altar outside the temple. There were fixed rules for exactly how to carry out a sacrifice.

Bronze figure of a boar being led to the sacrificial altar.

Altar from Hadrian's Wall in northern Britain, dedicated to 'Fortune, who brings you home' by a homesick soldier from north Africa.

In Rome the emperor was the head priest (*pontifex maximus*) of the state religion. He made sure everything was done correctly. Priests led the sacrificial animal, wearing beautiful ribbons or sashes, to the altar. The emperor, with part of his toga brought up to cover the top of his head, recited a prayer, using exactly the right words. Then the animal was killed, by having its skull smashed with an axe, or by having its throat cut with a special knife.

A bronze patera, *or sacrificial bowl.*

A bronze sacrificial knife.

VESTALS

One of the oldest and most important cults in Rome was the worship of Vesta, the goddess of the hearth and the home. Her round temple in the Forum contained the city's eternal flame.

The remains of the Temple of Vesta in the Roman Forum.

The seven priestesses of Vesta, the Vestals, were chosen from girls between the ages of six and ten. They served the goddess for at least thirty years. The Vestals had great power and public respect and they were given state bodyguards. Vestals had the right to buy and sell property, and were given the best seats at public events, for example at the theatre or the Colosseum.

The duties of the vestal princesses were to keep the sacred fire burning and make sacred cakes for the festivals of Rome's gods. They also had to promise to stay pure and untouched by a man. There were terrible punishments if they failed in their duty. If the fire went out the Vestals were whipped. If one of the Vestals was found with a man, the punishment was far worse.

Domitian ordered Cornelia, a chief Vestal, to be buried alive and her lovers to be clubbed to death.

Suetonius

Marble head of a Vestal.

MAGIC AND TELLING THE FUTURE

The Romans were very superstitious. They believed in magic and spells, and wore amulets and charms to keep away the evil eye.

People wanted to know what would happen in the future – and they had some very strange ways of finding out. A special priest called an *augur* watched the flights of birds. Another priest called a *haruspex* examined the insides of sacrificed animals – in particular the liver, feeling all the lumps and bumps! The priests claimed that this gave them special information about what was going to happen.

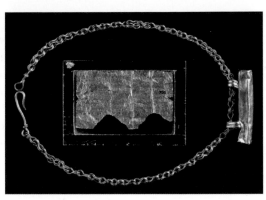

A gold charm and its carrying-case.

Romans also went to oracles, priestesses of the god Apollo, who foretold the future. In Italy there was an oracle called the *Sibyl* at Cumae, south of Rome. Tarquin, one of the early kings of Rome, bought three books of knowledge from her. Whenever Rome was in trouble people read these Sibylline books, to find out what to do.

> Augustus collected together all the prophecies and burnt over 2,000 of them. He kept only the Sibylline books and put them in two caskets under the statue of Apollo.
>
> Suetonius

WHO WERE THE PRIESTS?

High-ranking priests were amongst the most important people in society. But many ordinary people also served as priests and priestesses. Even children as young as six were chosen to train as priests of Isis and other gods.

In parts of the empire the emperor and his family were worshipped as living gods. This cult was run by priests called *Augustales*, usually ex-slaves or freedmen.

Tombstones and other sculptures sometimes show priests. Even if their title is not given we can often identify them by distinctive clothes, hairstyles, or objects they are wearing, such as headbands or wreaths.

Tombstone of the priest Antistius Sarculo and his wife (an ex-slave).

6 WOMEN

The role of women was very clear in Rome's early days. A woman was supposed to be the *matrona* – the keeper of the house. Women looked after the children and the men of the household. In early Rome there were harsh laws for women – a woman could be beaten if she was caught drinking alcohol.

Roman women were responsible for raising the children. As a result, this gave them a good deal of power, because Rome needed children, especially boys who would grow up into soldiers. Rome even gave special privileges and rewards to mothers of more than three children.

Women were citizens of Rome. They couldn't vote and couldn't stand for office but they were included in Roman society. They could be seen in everyday life, go out in public, take meals with their men and even attend meetings and public gatherings. Some of these rights and privileges seem to have been taken from the Etruscans, a people who had once lived north of Rome. In other parts of the ancient world, such as Greece, women were not allowed to be part of society or even to dine with men.

Carved gemstone showing a Roman matrona.

Statue of a Roman lady, probably set up as a grave monument.

MARRIAGE AND STATUS

At first, women had to rely on the authority of a male guardian, the *paterfamilias*, such as a father or uncle. Women could not make a will or sign contracts for selling or renting property. A girl could not choose her own husband, and when a woman married she passed into the hands of her husband and his family.

But choosing your wedding day was not easy. Weddings were forbidden in May, part of June and the first, ninth and fifteenth day of each month.

The bride and groom made a very public display of their coming together. Part of this was an important ceremony called the joining of the right hands – the *dextrarum iunctio*. The bride usually took with her a dowry – money or goods for her husband's family. Divorce was quite easy for a man – he simply took the wife back to her father's house and gave back the dowry.

Marble relief of a wedding. The bride and groom join hands.

WOMEN OF THE EMPIRE

As the republic came to an end and the empire began, women's lives became much freer. Because so many men were away fighting in Rome's armies, women had more control of the household, the family and their own affairs. It became easier for a woman to marry and to divorce, to own and inherit property and to make her own will. The role of women was transformed dramatically.

Women began to use their own independent incomes and became powerful members of everyday society. Just like rich men, they spent money on public buildings for their towns and paid for festivals and games. Some men did not like this!

> There's nothing more unbearable than a wealthy woman.
>
> Juvenal

Gradually the control of a male guardian became less and less important. In the early days of Rome, women were educated only to be good wives and mothers. They learnt domestic skills and how to manage the household. Later, some women demanded a broader education.

Marble head of Livia, the wife of Augustus.

Women read literature, science and mathematics and weren't afraid to show their knowledge in public. And women suddenly saw other women gaining real power. Livia, the wife of the first emperor Augustus, was a very influential woman. Some said she was the real power behind Augustus's throne. She was the first living woman to be as visible as any man. Her statues and her image on coins were seen all over the empire – the Roman world was no longer a world of men only. Livia was soon followed by the emperor's sister, then the emperor's daughter, and soon there were images of powerful women everywhere.

A wooden writing tablet from Vindolanda Fort near Hadrian's Wall. An officer's wife invites another lady to her birthday party.

WOMEN AT WORK

Roman writers usually only wrote about women in their own class – the nobility. But of course most Roman women were not upper class.

To find out about ordinary women, we have to look at archaeology. Gravestones are very interesting sources of information. They show women involved in the hands-on running of everything from butcher's shops to pubs and taverns. Other pictures of women, for example wall-paintings and mosaics from the cities of Pompeii and Herculaneum, show them with their husbands, sometimes running the family business. The new Roman woman had arrived.

Part of a wall painting from Pompeii showing a man and a woman.

Marble bust of Antonia, the mother of the emperor Claudius.

Wall painting from Pompeii showing a businessman, Paquius Proculus, and his wife.

HAIR AND BEAUTY

Sheer beauty is power.

Juvenal

Roman women of all levels in society understood that their appearance was very important. A rich woman had several servants for this, including an *ornatrix* to dress her hair and put on her make-up. Hairstyles changed, just as they do today, and people wanted the most fashionable look. At the time of the emperor Augustus, hairstyles were very simple, but a hundred years later women had big walls of curls (made using heated metal rollers) and big plaits of hair coiled into huge buns at the back of their heads.

Bone comb carved with the name of its owner, Modestina.

Gold coin showing Faustina, the wife of Antoninus Pius. Women often copied the hairstyles they saw on imperial portraits.

Marble bust of Olympias with a hairstyle typical of about AD 100.

Marble statue of a young woman wearing pleated robes and a waved wig.

Make-up was very popular – but some of the ingredients were awful. Pale skin was essential for a rich woman. White face powder was made from clay or, worse, from white lead – a very poisonous substance that ate into the skin.

Lipstick and powdered rouge or 'blusher' were made from mulberries, grapes or red lead. (Red lead was just as poisonous as the white stuff.) Eye-liner was often made of pure soot. When you took your make-up off, the best face cream was made of barley, narcissus bulbs and ground-up deer antlers. Before you went to bed you could brush your teeth with a toothpaste with a special ingredient – urine ...

> When you go to sleep, your face doesn't sleep with you. It sleeps in bottles and jars on your cabinet.
>
> Martial

Painted mummy portrait showing a beautiful, wealthy lady from Roman Egypt.

Many Italian women had dark hair, but some women wanted hair that was even darker, so they imported jet-black hair all the way from India, or dyed their hair. One recipe for black dye involved soaking dead leeches in wine for a month! Other women wanted blond or red hair so they spent a fortune on wigs made with hair from German or British women.

7 Soldiers and Sailors

The Roman army, led by its commander in chief the emperor, was an amazing fighting machine – the most successful of all time! It was vitally important to the success and stability of the empire.

> 'My sons, pay the troops, look after your brother, and forget about everyone else.'
>
> The emperor Septimius Severus

At first the army was made up of farmers, who worked their land for part of the year and served in the army for the other part. As the empire grew bigger and needed more troops, there were more career soldiers, who stayed in the army for many years.

Bust of the emperor Antoninus Pius wearing military clothes.

THE ARMY

The main division of the army was the legion, or *legio*.

There were about 5,000 men in a legion, divided into centuries of 80 men (like the company in today's army). Each legion also had about 5,000 auxiliaries, non-citizens who provided specialized units, such as archers or cavalry.

After twenty-five years in the army, auxiliaries were granted Roman citizenship. In about AD 200 the Roman army numbered around 300,000 men, in thirty-three legions with their auxiliaries.

A legionary soldier wearing armour made of metal plates, the lorica segmentata.

An auxiliary wearing a leather tunic and leggings.

A ROMAN AUXILIARY

This bronze diploma was awarded to an auxiliary cavalryman called Gemellus. He had served in Britain, and when he retired after twenty-five years service, he went back to his home in Pannonia (Hungary), where the diploma was found. Gemellus's reward for his long service was Roman citizenship for himself, his wife and children.

The diploma lists the auxiliary units that were in Britain at this time. They came from all over the empire, from Spain and Africa, Germany, Hungary and Greece. Gemellus retired in AD 122, the year Hadrian visited Britain and ordered the building of Hadrian's Wall.

Roman cavalry sword, longer than the infantry gladius.

MILITARY TECHNOLOGY

Rome's success was due to the discipline and training of its troops, but also to some technological advances. Legionary soldiers wore fairly light, very protective armour made of flexible metal plates stitched together. Machines were used for besieging cities or for fighting enemies in the field. These included the *ballista*, which fired large, armour-piercing bolts with great force and speed, and the *onager* ('donkey'), which hurled rocks great distances. The *testudo* (tortoise) was a manoeuvre in which legionary soldiers linked shields over their heads and moved forward like a tank!

Modern re-enactors performing the testudo.

We know so much about the Roman army and its tactics thanks to the carvings on Trajan's Column in Rome.

This great monument was put up by the emperor Trajan around AD 100 to celebrate his conquest of Dacia (Romania). The carvings that spiral up to the top show the story of the campaign. There are very detailed pictures of soldiers marching, cheering the emperor, crossing rivers, besieging cities and fighting the enemy.

ARMY SETTLEMENTS

As a Roman army advanced it set up small marching camps. When an area was settled, the soldiers established permanent bases called *castra*.

A *castrum* was laid out on a standard grid, with a main east-west street, the *Decumanus*, and a north-south street, the *Cardo*. It was like a small city. As well as military activities, the army ran industries producing bricks, tiles and pottery. *Castra* often grew into big civilian settlements. The names of British cities such as Lan<u>caster</u>, <u>Chester</u> and Glou<u>cester</u> include a version of the word *castrum*, showing Roman military origins. The army built border defences such as Hadrian's Wall, and also built and maintained roads, bridges and aqueducts.

Mask worn by a Roman cavalryman at parades and special events.

Reconstructed gate at the Roman fort of Arbeia (modern South Shields) in northern Britain.

SOLDIERS ABROAD

Soldiers came from all over the empire and were often posted far from home. Wherever they went, the soldiers had a huge impact on the local area. Their Latin language began to spread amongst the local people. Roman fashions in clothing and housing began to catch on.

> I have sent you sandals from Sattua, two pairs of socks, and two pairs of underpants.
>
> A letter to a soldier serving at Vindolanda fort near Hadrian's Wall.

Wooden writing tablet from Vindolanda with a letter about socks and underpants.

Soldiers' pay packets brought money into the local economy. Some very common English words linked to money come from the Roman army. The word 'soldier' comes from the Latin word *solidi*, the gold coins used to pay soldiers. 'Salary' comes from the word *sal* (salt), because some of a legionary's pay came in the form of a salt ration. But influences worked both ways. Some Roman soldiers began to adopt local ways, especially religion. Soldiers also started to marry local women, increasing the blending and diversity of the empire and its people.

A gold solidus *coin of the emperor Constantius.*

Ceremonial military robes from Roman Egypt, made from crocodile skin.

THE ROMAN NAVY

In Rome's early years, when she was conquering Italy, the navy was not very important. But when Rome expanded into the lands around the Mediterranean, she needed ships. The fleet really became important when Rome fought Carthage, a powerful north African city, in the third century BC. Rome finally defeated the Carthaginian navy in 260 BC, opening up the Mediterranean.

The sea was the easiest way to link Rome's territories, from Spain to Egypt. The navy (*classis*) fought powerful foreign states and gangs of pirates. There were several Roman fleets, stationed at different naval bases – Alexandria for the eastern Mediterranean, Misenum on the Bay of Naples for the centre. Other important fleets patrolled the Danube and Rhine rivers, and another, the *Classis Britannicus*, was based in Britain.

> When the Romans saw that the war against the Carthaginians was dragging on, they decided for the first time to build ships, but their shipwrights were completely unused to building warships. However, one Carthaginian warship ran aground and into the hands of the Romans. They used this ship as a model to build their entire fleet.
>
> Polybius

One of the most important battles in Roman history was fought at sea off the coast of Greece. In 31 BC Mark Antony and the Egyptian queen Cleopatra were completely defeated at the sea battle of Actium by Octavian. Octavian gained control of the Roman world. He took the title 'Augustus', and the Roman empire began.

Decorative front (prow) of a Roman ship found very near Actium.

8 SLAVES AND FREEDMEN

Slaves are people who are owned by someone else. Millions of slaves (men, women and children) lived in Rome and Italy. Today we hate the idea of slavery, but to the Romans it was normal.

'People tell me you're kind to your slaves. I'm glad. They're human beings like us.'
Some people say 'But they're slaves!'
'Well, I prefer to call them friends. Poor, but friends.'

Seneca

Some people were born as slaves, others were prisoners of war, or were condemned by the Roman courts to hard labour in mines or quarries. These slaves were often kept in chains and treated very badly. Greece and other Greek-speaking countries in the Mediterranean provided many slaves, as did Gallia (modern France), Hispania (modern Spain) and Britain.

Don't buy too many slaves from the same country. They'll only squabble.

Pliny

Tag of a slave (or perhaps an animal) saying that the wearer should be returned to his owner if he got lost.

Silver pepperpot in the shape of a young slave, asleep.

HARD WORK

Many slaves worked on farms. Rome and the other big cities needed huge quantities of food and drink, and most of it came from large estates. Slaves did all the work.

Wheat for Rome's bread came from Sicily and Egypt. Olive oil for food, soap and lighting the empire's lamps came from north Africa and Spain. Wine came from huge vineyards in Italy. Slaves often did hard or dirty work in the towns, too, constructing buildings and working in leather and wool factories and in laundries.

Because they were the property of their masters, slaves were sometimes badly treated.

Bronze figure of a man ploughing with two oxen.

> If the mistress of the house is in a filthy mood because there is a curl out of place, then the slave girl who is doing her hair will have her own hair torn, her tunic ripped and she will be beaten with a strap.
>
> Juvenal

But life was not always bad if you were a slave. They were sometimes valued members of the household, working as teachers, cooks, librarians, gardeners or accountants. Others were artists, such as sculptors and painters. Children of slaves were sometimes brought up alongside their master's children. When special slaves died they were commemorated with beautiful gravestones and were sometimes even buried in their master's family tomb.

Terracotta figurine of a slave, heavily laden with a sack, a basket and an amphora.

> Here lies Vitalis, slave of Gaius Lavius Faustus and also his son, a slave born in his home.
>
> From a gravestone found near Philippi, Greece

FREEDMEN AND WOMEN

A slave did not always live all his or her life as a slave in the Roman empire. It was possible to become a freedman or freedwoman. A freedman (*libertus*) or a freedwoman (*liberta*) was an ex-slave, who bought his freedom, earned it through good service or was freed in his owner's will.

The ex-master protected his freedman, who had to be helpful and loyal to him. This system was known as 'patronage'. As a sign of this bond, freedmen took part of their ex-master's name as their own.

Freedmen were not full Roman citizens, and were excluded from high positions in the army and civilian society, but they dominated certain professions in which their owners could not openly take part. They were the bankers, merchants, shippers, factory owners and artisans who ran the imperial economy. Many freedmen were skilled craftsmen, making everything from sculptures, jewellery or metalwork to pottery and glass.

Drinking cup made of fluorspar, a rare stone from Persia (Iran). Many of the finest works of art were made by slaves or freedmen.

Some freedmen made large fortunes, in particular those who ran their masters' businesses. Like other wealthy Romans, they built or restored public buildings, sponsored games, owned expensive villas and gave extravagant banquets. Even after their death they wanted to be remembered as good members of society, so they built expensive tombs, with sculpted reliefs or portraits, showing them and their families posing in their best clothing as proud Romans.

Gravestone of an ex-slave called Lucius Ampudius Philomusus, a corn importer, and his wife and daughter.

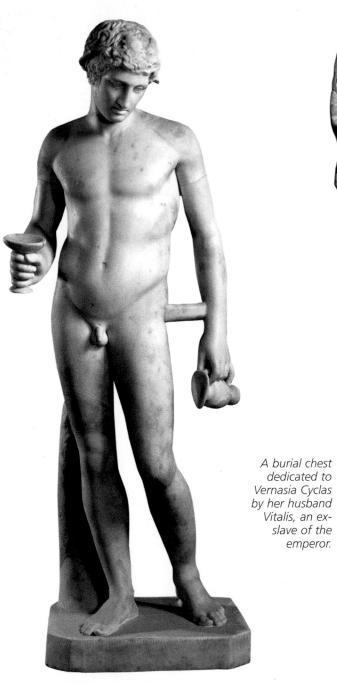

Marble statue of a young man, signed by the sculptor who made it: Marcus Cossutius Cerdo.

A burial chest dedicated to Vernasia Cyclas by her husband Vitalis, an ex-slave of the emperor.

VERNASIAE
CYCLADI
CONIVGIOPTIMAE
VIXANNXXVII
VITALIS·AVG·L
SCRIB · CVB

9 CHILDREN

Children were extremely important to the Romans – they were the future of the city. Boys grew up and joined the army, and girls grew up and gave birth to more boys.

A child's early years could be difficult. When a baby was born its mother gave it to the man of the house, the *paterfamilias*, so he could accept it into the family. At the beginning of Rome's history he sometimes refused. If the baby was a girl and he wanted a boy, the *paterfamilias* could leave the child out in the countryside to die, or sell it into slavery.

By the time of the empire this didn't happen any more. But there were other dangers. Many children died of infections and other disease, because the Romans didn't have the skills or the medicines to save them. Not even the imperial family was safe. In the second century AD the emperor Marcus Aurelius and his wife Faustina had twelve children, but less than half of them lived to grow up. It was important to have as many children as possible, so that at least some of them would survive.

Mummy of a little boy from Roman Egypt. The decoration shows that he was from a rich family.

Gravestones of children often show them as adults, making up for the grown-up life they never had.

Emperors passed laws rewarding women who had more than three children and punishing people who had none or who didn't get married. The emperor Trajan set up a special welfare system to feed poor and orphaned children in Italy. The citizens of the future had to be protected.

A gravestone from Hadrian's Wall of a little boy who died aged six. He is shown as a grown-up charioteer.

A burial chest for two little boys from Rome. It says that one of them received free corn from the government.

THE NAMING CEREMONY

When they were eight or nine days old, children were officially named at a ceremony called the *nominalia*. They were given a disc-shaped locket, or *bulla*, which contained an amulet or lucky charm. They wore these charms until they became adults.

A statuette of a young child in a walking frame, wearing a bulla.

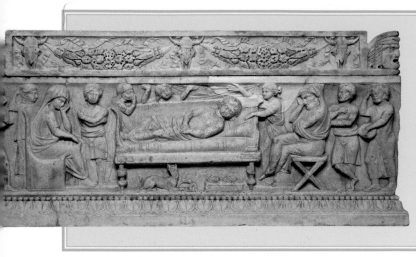

A FUNERAL

This stone burial chest, or sarcophagus, was made for a little girl who died in about AD 200. She is shown resting on soft pillows on a couch, as if she was just sleeping. At the ends of the bed are her mother and father. All around are people mourning her. They may be members of the family, or professional mourners that Romans used to hire to weep and wail at funerals. Under her bed are her slippers and her faithful pet dog.

SCHOOL AND WORK

In the richer families both boys and girls went to elementary schools. Here they learned the basics of reading and writing in Latin and sometimes Greek, and mathematics.

A girl's formal education usually finished when she was about eleven or twelve. Then she started to learn from her mother how to run the home and look after a family. Boys remained at school, learning skills such as speech-making. They also learned to ride a horse, had military training to prepare them for the army, and were often sent travelling abroad. All of this helped to make them ready for life as a Roman citizen.

Some children started public work very young. Some very young children were chosen to be priests and priestesses. For example, children under ten could be priestesses of Vesta or Isis. But if they lived, most children enjoyed a normal childhood.

A marble relief showing a young man training a horse.

Marble bust of a young boy. His hairstyle suggests that he was a follower of the Egyptian goddess Isis.

TOYS AND GAMES

Playing was a very important part of childhood in Rome, just as it is now. There were lots of different toys. Very young children had rattles, called *crepundia*, and little charms, or bells and whistles in the form of birds and animals.

Older children had dolls made of terracotta, rags and wood. Some dolls had moveable arms and legs and sometimes they had miniature furniture such as beds and chairs. There were also little figures of gladiators, actors, slaves and soldiers – people that children saw in everyday life. There were all sorts of animal figures made of terracotta, wood and even lead (which was very poisonous – so let's hope small children didn't put them in their mouths!). Some of these animals were on wheels so they could be dragged or raced along. Children used the animals to play at peaceful farming or to recreate the terrible fights and battles of the arena.

Other toys included spinning tops, dice, knucklebones and even yo-yos. Children and adults also played board games, with special counters or with pebbles, nuts and marbles.

Children played games of chase, blind man's buff or piggy-back and also games with balls made of stuffed leather or bundles of cloth. There were some team games but nothing as organized as modern football, rugby, basketball or cricket.

Rag dolls were popular with children all over the empire. This one survived because it was buried in the hot, dry sands of Egypt.

A wooden model of a horse that could be pulled along on its wheels.

A lead model of a camel.

GROWING UP

There was no set age for officially becoming an adult, but generally by fourteen or fifteen years old boys and girls were full members of society. We don't know very much about the ceremonies that celebrated a girl becoming a woman. Most histories at this time were written by men for men, and sadly they weren't interested in girls.

His father was his reading teacher, his law teacher ... and taught his son to hurl the javelin, fight in armour and ride a horse.

Plutarch

Sarcophagus of a child showing young boys playing games.

Painted portrait of a young girl from Egypt.

Marble statue of a boy wearing a child's toga and a hulla (locket).

When a boy became a man, it meant that Rome was gaining a new full citizen and a new soldier, so the ceremony could be very grand. The boy took off his locket (*bulla*) and dedicated it to the household gods. Then he swapped his childhood toga, with its coloured border, for the pure white toga of a man.

Afterwards the father led his son to the Forum, together with all the men of the family and all his most powerful and influential friends. Here, the boy's name was added to the list of citizens. This was the most important part of the day. The family gave thanks to the gods and then there was a huge banquet at the family home. The boy was now a man.

10 FARMERS AND FOODMAKERS

Farmers were very important in the Roman world. Much of the population lived and worked on the land. Farming was not always a full-time job, however. Farmers also served as soldiers, fighting for part of the year and farming for the rest of the year.

Rome began as a small town, and family farms in and around Rome provided all the food and drink that the people needed. These farms had plots of vegetables, fruit orchards and fields of wheat and barley to produce flour for bread. Little vineyards made wine, and local farmers and shepherds raised sheep, cattle, goats and pigs in the surrounding countryside.

Oil lamp with a picture of a shepherd and his flock under a tree.

Stone relief showing people boiling wine to make defrutum, *a thicker and sweeter drink.*

Some people went out into the forests and hunted animals such as deer and wild boar.

But by about 100 BC Rome had conquered all of Italy, and her population had grown to over half a million people. The small farms couldn't produce enough food and drink, so farming changed.

A mosaic from North Africa showing an animal hunt.

Bronze statuette of a bull. The Romans preferred to use cattle for work (pulling carts) and so they did not eat very much beef.

A mosaic from Italy showing different types of sea creatures. The artist used very small mosaic cubes, so the picture looks very detailed.

In many parts of the empire, such as north Africa, Italy and Spain, rich landowners bought up the little farms and put them together to make enormous estates called *latifundia*.

These estates produced massive quantities of wheat, olive oil and wine, and were so big that the only way to run them was with slave labour. There were plenty of slaves around from Rome's victories in countries such as Greece and Spain. Some estates specialized in rearing large numbers of pigs or sheep – the first factory farms!

Near the coast, huge fish farms produced tons of fresh or salted fish and fish sauce (*garum*).

GARUM

Garum was a fish sauce, usually made from tuna or mackerel. To make *garum* you took the heads, tails, intestines, and bones of the fish and left them in big stone tanks with plenty of salt to ferment under the hot sun. The factories smelt awful, but the Romans loved *garum* and used it in starters, main courses and even puddings!

A novelty bottle in the shape of a fish. Fish was a popular food all over the empire.

Silver bowl with fine decoration. Rich Romans liked to use silver plates and cups.

Often poor people couldn't afford the most basic foods, so Roman emperors organized cheap – or sometimes free – handouts of bread, oil and sometimes pork. On special occasions, like the emperor's birthday, they even gave out wine. People could also go to a street corner bar or tavern to buy cheap meals such as soups, pies and sausages.

The inside of a thermopolium, *or tavern, in Ostia.*

Rich people's food was different. They had their own kitchens and cooks, often Greek slaves or servants.

Wealthy families competed to see who could serve the most extravagant meals or had the biggest set of silver tableware. The senate passed laws limiting the number of silver plates and banning exotic foods. One of these foods was the dormouse, a plump little mouse that Romans fattened up in special pottery jars.

Bronze statuette of a mouse eating a nut.

ROMAN FEASTS

But Roman meals became bigger and more spectacular. Some emperors served meals with over twenty-five courses. We know what rich Romans ate because we can read a recipe book written by Apicius who lived in Rome at the time of Nero in the 50s – 60s AD.

For starters there were vegetables, eggs, cheese, snails, seafood, fish, chicken, duck and, of course, dormouse! For the main course Romans ate meat, especially goat, pork and wild boar. Apicius also gives recipes for exotic dishes like flamingo and parrot. To finish, the Romans loved puddings – including one called *libum* that was just like cheesecake. But most important was fruit, especially apples, peaches, grapes, cherries, figs and dates.

Wall painting of a wicker basket of big, juicy figs. Even the seeds are shown.

The Romans were messy eaters and by the end of the meal, the floor was covered in the bits and pieces they had dropped, from lettuce leaves to fruit pips.

RECIPES

The Romans loved exotic recipes. Dormouse should be

> stuffed with pork mince, dormouse meat, pepper, pine nuts and *garum*, rolled in honey and poppy-seeds and fried.

The best *garum* was

> … made from the blood of a mackerel that is still gasping

and the best way to serve a parrot is in a sauce made from

> vinegar, honey, onion, sesame seed and dates.

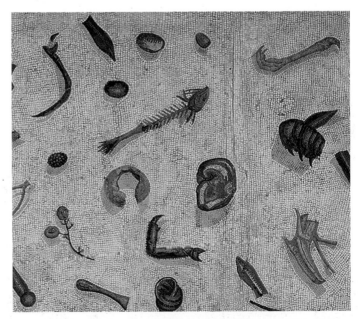

Mosaic from a dining room, showing the floor covered in food after a meal – everything from crab claws to fruit pips.

11 MERCHANTS AND TRADERS

The Roman empire was vast, with many cities and towns. These cities became richer and bigger as the empire expanded, but this created a problem. How could the emperor make sure the cities were supplied with all the goods they needed? Through an army of merchants, traders and shopkeepers!

Many merchants and tradesmen were freedmen (ex-slaves). They set up tombstones and other monuments, proudly showing the trades and skills that had allowed them to become wealthy and enter Roman society.

The Mediterranean was at the centre of Rome's empire and it became a superhighway, criss-crossed by thousands of ships carrying all sorts of cargoes.

Stone relief showing an ox cart entering a city. It is carrying a huge animal skin filled with wine.

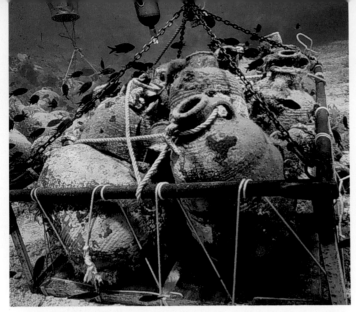

Amphorae (oil or wine jars) discovered on a Roman shipwreck in the Mediterranean.

Stone relief showing a man steering a small merchant ship.

Food was the biggest and most important cargo. For bread, merchants loaded ships with enormous quantities of corn from Egypt, Sicily and north Africa. Wine came from Italy and the eastern Mediterranean. Olive oil for eating, cooking and for making soap came from north Africa and Spain. Food and liquids were transported in huge ships – the equivalent of our super-tankers.

> I decided to go into business and built five ships, loaded them with wine and sent them to Rome ... All the ships sank ... So I built bigger ones and filled them with wine, bacon, beans, perfume and slaves. Now I've built a house and bought slaves and cattle.   Petronius

THE SIZE OF TRADE

Because Rome was so big it needed enormous amounts of imported goods. Roman shipwrecks found near France and Italy are full of large clay jars for liquids, *amphorae* – some have over 5,000 amphorae on board. Today in Rome we can see real proof of just how big and important trade was between the city and its empire. In the south of Rome there is a hill called Monte Testaccio. It is about fifty metres high and one hundred and seventy metres long. But this isn't one of Rome's famous seven hills. This hill was entirely man-

made! Its name means 'old pot hill' and the hill is built entirely of broken and dumped *amphorae* used to bring olive oil to Rome from Spain and north Africa. The Romans really had a very modern economy.

The companies who managed Roman trade were very organized. At major ports such as Alexandria in Egypt, Carthage in Africa (modern Tunisia) or Pozzuoli or Ostia in Italy, there were specially-built customs houses, import-export offices and enormous warehouses for storing goods.

In Ostia the shipping companies, especially the corn importers, were mostly based in a square behind the theatre, called Company Square.

Mosaic from Company Square, Ostia, showing an oil amphora with two palm trees.

Bronze coin showing Ostia, the bustling port of Rome.

Red slip-ware bowl from Tunisia. Imports like these travelled with the big cargoes of oil, corn and wine.

Each office had a mosaic floor that showed which part of the Roman empire they traded with. Other merchants brought luxury goods, such as fine fabrics, spices, or exotic animals and, sadly, even people. Once the goods arrived at the ports they were distributed and sold across Italy and the empire. Raw materials and finished goods went to craftsmen and shopkeepers. Just like today, shops came in all shapes and sizes and the streets of all the towns and cities of the empire were filled with them, selling everything from food and clothing to furniture, metal goods and luxuries such as jewellery. Very often the shopkeeper was also the craftsman. He made things in his workshop, sold them in the shop, and lived in the rooms above.

There's a bookshop near the Forum of Caesar with adverts for poetry books pasted all over it.

Martial

A set of bronze scales.

WEIGHTS AND MEASURES

The government realized that the people of the empire, especially the poor, were very dependent on shops for their food. So to stop shopkeepers cheating, they organized sets of standard weights and measures in every major town and city. Some emperors even tried to set price limits on essential things like bread, wine and pork.

MALLS AND MARKETS

In Rome, of course, shops were bigger and better than elsewhere in the empire. Very expensive, boutique-like shops were set under the arches of the great covered basilicas in the Roman Forum, and the emperor Trajan built a massive complex of shops and offices as part of his new Forum. The curved front of part of the markets can still be seen today. There are great covered halls, five levels of shops and offices. Even roads were included in the design, so you could drive away with your shopping!

Market stalls could be found all over the Roman world. Sometimes they were fixed, but mostly stall-holders travelled around, like today, from town to town on market days and holidays. The Romans had very complex calendars to work out market days. Archaeologists in Pompeii have found lists of places and dates scratched on the walls, to remind people of the market days in different places.

There were stalls all around places like the Colosseum on fight days, selling food and souvenirs.

The multi-storey 'shopping centre' of Trajan's market in Rome.

The ruins of a public bakery in Pompeii, with an oven and several mills for grinding corn.

12 CRAFTSMEN AND ARTISTS

Rome's culture and art were based on Greece, but the Romans didn't just copy Greek ideas. Instead they gave them a Roman twist.

Gravestone of two craftsmen, a maker of coins and a carpenter, with pictures of their tools.

An Etruscan sarcophagus. The Romans often used Etruscan craftsmen.

Early in Rome's history, many of the city's artists and craftsmen who made beautiful objects out of terracotta and metal came from Etruria to the north of Rome.

After Rome conquered the lands around the Mediterranean she took ideas and craftsmen from the Greek world.

Dozens of workshops sprang up in Rome, making beautiful objects out of stone, bronze, silver, glass, ivory and amber. The names on signed artworks are often Greek, so we know that they often came from Greece.

MOSAICS

The Romans loved mosaics and wall paintings and put them in their houses and temples. Mosaics were invented by the Greeks, who made them from stone cubes called *tesserae*. The Romans started to use glass cubes, which were much lighter, so they could put mosaics on the walls and even ceilings.

A Roman mosaic with Dionysus and his panther.

The temple of Hercules in Rome. It was built by Greek craftsmen using the finest Greek marble.

PAINTINGS AND STATUES

Wall painting from Pompeii showing the Greek hero Odysseus and the Sirens.

The Romans first saw wall paintings in Greek lands and soon adopted them. Greeks used simple blocks of bright colour, but the Romans added panels showing scenes from Greek mythology, or daily life in the city. They even painted the ceilings of their rooms. The houses of well-off Romans were very colourful!

The Romans also put thousands of statues into their houses, public buildings and squares.

They wanted the best – and that meant Greek. Rich people could bring back original bronze or marble sculptures from Greece. But if the original had already gone you could get a copy made. Many sculpture workshops sprang up, copying statues of gods and heroes. Walking round Rome you could see twenty copies of the same statue of Venus, fifteen Apollos and dozens of images of Hercules.

Roman marble statue of a discus-thrower, copied from a Greek bronze original.

JEWELLERY

Jewellery was very popular everywhere. Some fashions were universal. Women from Egypt to Britain wore snake-shaped bracelets, gold ball earrings and crescent-shaped pendants.

The empire's trade links brought exotic gems and jewels from far beyond its frontiers.

A mummy portrait from Roman Egypt showing a Roman lady wearing fine gold jewellery.

A hooped earring threaded with pearls.

Brooches, finger rings and earrings were set with imported gemstones such as blue sapphires and purple amethysts from Sri Lanka and milky white pearls from India.

SILVER

One of the finest of the Roman arts was silver-working. Workshops in Italy produced sets of silver tableware for rich people.

A silver drinking set.

GLASS AND POTTERY

Artists didn't just work for the rich – even poorer people could use beautiful things. During the time of the empire fine pottery and glass became available, even to the not so rich. Glass had been invented thousands of years before, but the Romans invented glass-blowing.

Part of a pottery mould used for making red slip-ware pottery in Italy.

Glass-blowing meant that bottles, cups and jars could be made quickly and cheaply. Pottery was also mass-produced in moulds, in workshops in Italy, France and north Africa.

A glass beaker decorated to look like silver.

The most popular pottery, called red slip-ware, had a nice shiny red surface. It was made in Italy, France and Tunisia and was exported all over the empire and beyond. It has even been found in India.

On the table red-ware has a high reputation. It is made in Arezzo in Italy and Spain and Turkey … it is carried far across the seas.

Pliny

Each set contained drinking cups, plates for serving and eating and other vessels including jugs and strainers (for getting the bits out of wine). There were also pepper pots for serving valuable Indian spices, and small silver statuettes of gods and goddesses to protect the diners while they were eating.

A small statuette of the goddess Fortuna. Above her head are the gods of the days of the week.

Red slip-ware chalice decorated with pictures of the four seasons.

13 ACTORS AND PERFORMERS

The Romans loved going to the theatre. They enjoyed plays written many years before by Greeks – the tragedies (sad stories) of Euripides, or the comedies (funny stories) of Menander. They also loved comedies by Roman writers, and plays rather like pantomimes.

One of the earliest Roman playwrights was a man called Plautus, who lived in about 220 BC. He wrote comedies in the Greek style, but gave them some Roman characters, such as the clever slave, the big-headed soldier, the silly old man and the modest girl. About twenty of Plautus's plays survived. The English writer William Shakespeare copied some of Plautus' plots and characters for his own comedies.

Bone figure of an actor holding his mask.

Terracotta figurine of an actor wearing a mask.

THEATRES

Every major town and city had a theatre. They were large semicircular buildings, often the biggest structure in the city. Theatres were solidly constructed of stone, brick and concrete. Many theatres still stand today because after the empire ended they were reused as houses or forts. The semicircle of seats, or *cavea*, was very steep so that everyone could get a good view. The centre of the action was the stage – the *scaena*, with a stage building or *scaenae frons* two or three storeys high, decorated with marble columns and statues. The actors appeared out of three different doorways, creating funny and confusing comings and goings.

The theatre at Ostia.

Hadrian, in honour of his predecessor Trajan, ordered the theatre seats to be sprayed with perfume.

Historia Augusta

In Greek and Roman plays actors wore distinctive costumes and masks, to tell the audience which character they were. To make the actors easier to see they wore shoes with platform soles! The most common masks showed faces with exaggerated smiles for happy or lucky characters, and huge frowns for unhappy or angry ones.

Stone carving of a theatre mask.

In Greece, the theatre was part of a festival for the god Dionysus (Roman Bacchus), so actors were very important. But the Romans thought acting was not respectable at all. Women were not allowed to be actors, so all women's parts were played by men. Nobody from the aristocracy could become an actor, and the Romans passed laws that prevented actors from taking part in public life. But this didn't stop the emperor Nero.

Nero made his stage debut at Naples. He sang and sang and did not stop, even when an earthquake rocked the theatre.

Suetonius

While he (Nero) sang, no one could leave the theatre even in an emergency. Some women had to give birth there, others leapt out over the outside wall, or even pretended they had died.

Suetonius

MUSIC

Music accompanied the action during performances in the theatre. In fact, music was a vital part of every important event, from weddings, funerals and religious ceremonies, to shows in the theatre, arena and circus.

A mosaic from Pompeii showing a band of street musicians.

There were also groups of musicians who went from town to town playing popular and traditional music.

Wall paintings, mosaics and sculptures show what Roman musical instruments looked like. Archaeologists have found the remains of some real instruments. Wind instruments included two different types of trumpet – the large circular *cornu*, taken over from the Etruscans, and the long straight *tuba*. Both trumpets were also used by the army to give signals in battle.

A bronze cornu.

Stone relief of a young man playing the aulos.

The Romans also used the Greek flute (*aulos* or *tibia*), which was sometimes played in pairs. For percussion the Romans used drums, the tambourine (*tympanum*), castanets and the rattle (*sistrum*).

The most complex instrument of all was the organ, with a series of pipes of different sizes and lengths that made a range of noises when air was pushed through them. Roman organs used water to increase the pressure and make the sounds.

Stringed instruments were popular. One was the lute – the ancestor of the modern guitar. The oldest and most famous was the lyre. This had a sound-box and two tall arms which supported the crossbar to which the strings were attached.

The Romans preferred a heavy version of the lyre called a *kithara*, because it gave a louder and more wide-ranging sound. This was a favourite instrument for artists and musicians and it was the instrument that the emperor Nero used to accompany his songs and poetry.

Terracotta figure of man playing the water organ.

Bronze statuette of a dwarf playing the castanets and dancing.

14 CHARIOTEERS

Chariot racing was the most popular form of entertainment in the Roman world, after gladiator fights. At first, chariot races were held on holy days as part of religious ceremonies. Gradually people came to expect more and more races and they became part of the normal calendar of events.

> All Rome is at the circus today.
>
> Juvenal

Legend says that the first races in Rome were held by Rome's first king, Romulus, in the valley below the Palatine Hill. About a hundred years later another king, Tarquin, built the first fixed race-track, called a 'circus'. The circus had a very special shape, long and thin with one flat end and one rounded end.

The Circus Maximus was the largest and most important of Rome's five public circuses for chariot and horse racing. In fact, it was the biggest structure for spectacular entertainment in the empire. It was 600 m long and 180 m wide and could hold almost 200,000 spectators on more than 30 km of seating.

Racing chariots were very light, not like the great heavy chariots sometimes seen on films and television. They were built for speed, and there were several different types. Charioteers raced in everything from a two-horse chariot (*biga*) to a twelve-horse monster! But their favourite was the four-horse chariot, the *quadriga*.

Bronze model of a biga, a two-horse chariot.

THE CIRCUS MAXIMUS

The Roman writer Juvenal famously remarked:

> ... the people of Rome crave only two things, bread and circuses.

Politicians knew how important the Circus was, so they spent a lot of money improving it to keep people happy (and for their own glory). Julius Caesar rebuilt most of the Circus Maximus in stone and the emperor Augustus added a royal box to give the imperial family a grandstand view from the Palatine Hill. The upper tier, still made of wood, was damaged by fire on several occasions. Rome's most famous fire – the Great Fire of Nero in AD 64 - started in the small shops and taverns huddled around the Circus. The wooden parts of the Circus collapsed completely in about AD 300, during Diocletian's reign, and writers reported that over 10,000 people were killed.

Down the centre of the track ran the central reserve, or *spina*, crammed with temples, shrines and other monuments, including two colossal obelisks brought from Egypt.

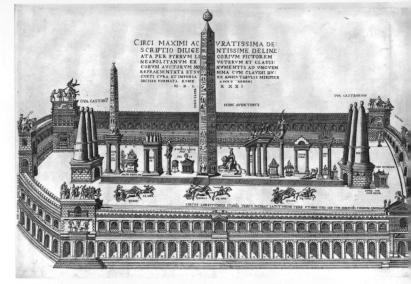

A print of 1581 showing an imaginary reconstruction of the Circus Maximus in Rome.

A normal race was seven laps around the track – a full distance of about six kilometres (four miles).

On each end of the *spina* was a huge turning-post (*meta*), with a clever way of telling the charioteers (and the audience) how many laps had been completed. At one end were seven huge bronze eggs, and at the other end were seven bronze dolphins, which dipped at the end of each lap.

Terracotta plaque showing a quadriga, a four-horse chariot. This was the Romans' favourite kind of racing chariot.

An oil lamp with chariots rushing out of the starting gates in the Circus Maximus.

TEAMS AND FANS

At a race, emotions ran very high. The excited crowd supported four different chariot teams. Each team wore coloured jackets – red, white, green and blue. Everyone felt close to the action. There were dozens of off-track entertainments, too. Food and drink sellers strolled through the aisles, and gamblers laid bets on the race results, and. Even the emperors liked to bet.

There were other, more romantic attractions. When the emperor Vespasian built the Colosseum it had a rigid seating system – women could only sit in the very top seats. But at the Circus, men and women could sit together. The writer Ovid, in his *Arts of Love*, said the Circus was a wonderful place to meet girls.

Go to the circus … you can sit close to her … find out her favourite horse, then back it yourself … 'Helpfully' brush the dust from her robes (even if they are not dusty) … plump up her cushion … protect her from the elbows and knees of fellow spectators … and offer to fan her with your programme. You're bound to find love in that crowd.

Many images of charioteers survive, showing them wearing distinctive banded and padded jackets and special caps – perhaps like modern crash helmets. During a race the charioteer wrapped the reins of the horses around his waist to help guide them. He carried a sharp knife so he could cut the reins and jump free if his chariot crashed. The sport was very dangerous, but prize money for races in the Circus Maximus could be huge. A gravestone in Rome commemorates Gaius Appuleius Diocles, a charioteer from Lusitania (modern Portugal). He competed in over 4,000 races in the early second century AD and built up an enormous fortune.

Ivory statuette of a charioteer wearing a banded jacket and carrying a palm branch of victory.

THE 'RACE OF LIFE'

The crowd adored charioteers.

Chariot racing was so popular that people used scenes of races, chariots, or even just the winning horses to decorate everyday objects. Oil lamps, floor mosaics and even burial chests (*sarcophagi*) were covered in action-filled scenes of chariots thundering around the track. Sometimes they were very realistic, but they could be pure fantasy, showing chariots driven by cupids or even monkeys! On burial chests scenes of chariots racing had a special importance, because writers and philosophers said that the race-track was a symbol of the continual race of our day to day lives.

A winning horse is celebrated on an oil lamp.

A lead burial chest showing a chariot.

Chariot racing remained popular until the end of the Roman empire. A Gaulish landowner called Rutilius Namatianus visited Rome in AD 416, six years after the city had been burnt by the barbarians. Even then, the games were still very popular. He said the roar of the crowd could be heard half way to the port at Ostia. The last recorded event was held around AD 540, after which there was no need for such a big circus – or any circus at all. The huge structure began to fall into ruins. In the Middle Ages the Circus was plundered for stone so that today only scraps of the structure survive. Now where a quarter of a million Romans used to scream and shout for their teams, all we can see is a huge green valley by the side of the Palatine Hill.

The remains of the Circus Maximus today.

15 GLADIATORS

Gladiators were the favourite entertainers of ancient Rome and are still loved today. For the crowds that came to the arena (or amphitheatre), gladiators were celebrities, just like our film and television stars, sports personalities and singers, all rolled into one.

Bronze helmet of a murmillo gladiator.

Maximus fights another gladiator and a tiger in the 2000 film Gladiator. *In reality, gladiators did not fight animals.*

Gladiators could be condemned criminals, prisoners of war and sometimes even volunteers. They were sent to a special military-style barracks for gladiators, a *ludus*. Once inside they were slaves, the property of their trainer (*lanista*). The training was very hard and the punishments extremely cruel, so why did people do it? Some wanted to win prizes, get rich and buy their freedom, others also wanted to be famous and loved by the people. Even some of the emperors, such as Commodus, liked to fight in the arena. People thought gladiators were very attractive.

> A senator's wife, Eppia, fell for a gladiator, Sergius. He was at least forty, with a bad arm, a scarred face and an eye oozing pus – but he was a gladiator. This made him seem *very* handsome.
>
> Juvenal

Gladiators fought on about thirty days in the year – more if the emperor wanted to celebrate a special event. Days in advance, painted advertisements were put on walls throughout the city, saying when the fights would be held, how many gladiators would compete, and who the sponsor was. Games needed rich sponsors because the animals, hunters and gladiators were very expensive.

Oil lamp showing an acrobat pole-vaulting over a bull. Acrobats performed in the arena before the gladiator fights.

THE COLOSSEUM

Gladiators fought in an amphitheatre, or arena – named after the Latin word for sand, *harena*. Sand was spread thickly on the floor to soak up all the blood. The largest and most famous arena in the empire was the Colosseum in Rome, which held about 70,000 people. Its ruins are still Rome's most recognizable structure. Seats were strictly reserved, with a special box for the imperial family. In the front rows were the priests and senators, then came the knights, other rich people, then the ordinary citizens and finally, right at the top, women and slaves.

The Colosseum, the largest arena in the empire.

A DAY AT THE ARENA

The day's events started with a grand parade, the *pompa*. Then came entertaining warm-up acts such as jugglers, acrobats and even performing animals. Monkeys fought in soldiers' uniforms and elephants balanced on their back legs or bowed down in front of the emperor. Then the mood changed as animals fought animals and afterwards animals fought men. These men were not gladiators, but hunters (*venatores*), specially trained animal-fighters.

> At Athens Hadrian put on a hunt of a thousand wild beasts.
>
> Historia Augusta

> When Titus opened his amphitheatre (the Colosseum) he exhibited (and killed) five thousand wild animals of all types in a single day.
>
> Suetonius

The morning finished with horribly cruel executions of criminals. These criminals (*noxii*), guilty of crimes such as murder or treason, were burned alive, crucified (nailed to wooden crosses) or thrown to the beasts. The prisoners who fought the beasts were untrained, and often in chains, so they stood no chance against wild and hungry animals. Then it was time to have lunch ...

A terracotta plaque of a panther attacking a venator *(hunter).*

Some of the people executed in the arena were Christians. Emperors such as Nero were very suspicious of the new religion, and they condemned thousands of Christians to die as *noxii*.

It was horribly cruel, but the bravery of the Christians, facing death for what they believed, inspired many others to desert the Roman gods.

HEROES OF THE ARENA

In the afternoon came the gladiators. The crowds had seen plenty of blood already, so with the gladiators they wanted to see skill and bravery. There were different types of gladiators, with special armour, who were trained to fight in a particular way. The *murmillo* was fully armed with a large shield and a heavy helmet. He relied on his heavy armour for protection.

The gladiator he usually fought against was the *Thraex* (Thracian) more lightly armed, with long leg-guards, and a small shield. He had a very distinctive sword, with a curved end that could stab up behind his enemy's shield.

Many artists have been inspired by events in the Roman arena. This picture, The Christian Martyr's Last Prayer, *was painted by Jean-Léon Gérôme in 1883. It shows Christians about to be torn to pieces by lions and tigers.*

They were disguised in animal skins so that dogs tore them to pieces, they were tied to crosses or set on fire and used as human torches by night ...

Tacitus

Bronze figurine of a Thraex (Thracian gladiator).

Marble gravestone of a gladiator called Hilarus.

Glass drinking vessel – turn it upside down like this, and it becomes a secutor's helmet.

Base of a glass bowl, showing a retiarius (net fighter) called Stratonicus.

A *retiarius* (net-fighter) was almost unarmed, except for a metal shoulder guard, but he was fast and could catch opponents in his net and stab them with his three-pronged trident. His opponent the *secutor* (chaser) had a rather scary helmet with trident-proof eye-holes.

Fights didn't last for very long, because gladiators became exhausted or were wounded.
A gladiator could stop a fight by putting down his shield and raising his hand. The fight stopped and the emperor asked the audience what to do.

This nineteenth-century painting by Jean-Léon Gérôme is called Pollice Verso. The winning gladiator is asking the emperor whether to kill, or spare, his defeated opponent.

FEMALE GLADIATORS

Not all gladiators were men. The emperor Domitian organized fights between female gladiators at night, and illuminated the Colosseum with torches, while other women fought on chariots. A carved stone relief, now in the British Museum, shows two women, Amazon and Achillia. They fought as gladiators in Halicarnassus (now Bodrum in modern Turkey). Happily, the relief tells us they were both allowed to leave the arena alive.

If the gladiator had fought well the crowd shouted 'Mitte! Mitte!' (Let him go! Let him go!), and he left the arena with honour. If the crowd didn't like him they shouted 'Iugula! Iugula!' (Slit his throat! Slit his throat!). A clever emperor agreed with the crowd – if not, the people could get very angry and even riot. Thousands of gladiators died in the arena but many left it alive and enjoyed a comfortable retirement. Some even opened their own gladiator schools – preparing the next generation of fighters.

As spectators left the Colosseum they passed lots of stalls and shops selling souvenirs. You could buy a little clay figure or a lamp showing your favourite gladiator to remind you of your day out at the arena.

Terracotta figurine of a Thraex *and a* hoplomachus.

Oil lamp showing the final moments of a gladiator fight.

FIND OUT MORE

You can find out more about the Romans and the things they made on the British Museum website. Go to **www.britishmuseum.org** and click on 'Explore the British Museum'. You can explore galleries, search for people and objects, and find online tours and games.

Other books on the Romans for younger readers

Richard Abdy, *Pocket Dictionary of the Roman Army*, British Museum Press 2008

Peter Connolly, *Pompeii*, Oxford University Press, 1990

Mike Corbishley, *Illustrated Encyclopaedia of Ancient Rome*, British Museum Press 2003

Irving Finkel, *Games*, British Museum Press 2005 *(includes the Roman game Duodecim scripta)*

Judy Lindsay, *The Gladiator Activity Book*, British Museum Press 2004

Sam Moorhead, *Pocket Explorer: The Roman Empire*, British Museum Press 2008

Paul Roberts, *Pocket Dictionary of Roman Emperors*, British Museum Press 2006

Katharine Wiltshire, *Pocket Timeline of Ancient Rome*, British Museum Press 2005

Katharine Hoare, *V-Mail: Letters from the Romans at Vindolanda Fort near Hadrian's Wall*, British Museum Press 2008

Richard Woff, *Pocket Dictionary of Greek and Roman Gods and Goddesses*, British Museum Press 2003

Books for older readers

Alan K. Bowman, *Life and Letters on the Roman Frontier: Vindolanda and its People*, British Museum Press 2003

Lucilla Burn, *The British Museum Book of Greek and Roman Art*, British Museum Press 1991

Peter Connolly and Hazel Dodge, *The Ancient City: Life in Classical Athens and Rome*, Oxford University Press Inc, 2000

Ada Gabucci, *Ancient Rome: Art, Architecture and History*, British Museum Press 2002

Paul Roberts, *Mummy Portraits from Roman Egypt*, British Museum Press 2008

Christopher Scarre, *Chronicle of the Roman Emperors*, Thames and Hudson 1995

INDEX